ECONOMICS
FUNDAMENTALS FOR ADULTS

Second Edition

Thomas R. Miller
Palm Beach Atlantic University

Linus
Publications, Inc.

Published by Linus Publications, Inc.
Deer Park, NY 11729

ISBN 10: 1-60797-410-X

ISBN 13: 978-1-60797-410-9

Printed in the United States of America.

Print Numbers   5   4   3   2   1

INTRODUCTION

I am a teacher; well, to be a bit more precise, I am a college professor. While pursuing a dual career track for much of my life (I have also served in varying administrative capacities for non-profit organizations), I have served four separate educational institutions. My initial teaching experience, back in the early 1980's, occurred as both a part-time and then temporary, full-time instructor in the "adult program" at a local community college, and I have Palm Beach Atlantic University to thank for my last seven years as a full-time professor of economics and business finance courses in its MacArthur School of Leadership that is exclusively focused on the adult student. I look forward to many more years of service.

But, the history I have personally experienced is quite conclusive: colleges and universities dabbled with adult degree programs 30-40 years ago, and now adult degree programs are "everywhere." Many (most?) universities that primarily serve traditional age college students (18-22) have added a department for adult degree programs, some universities exist to exclusively serve the older student, and I believe the proliferation of online courses and degrees is a direct result of seeking to educate our adult population. Indeed, when I first began writing this textbook, geared for adult students, the prevailing statistic was that 10 million "older" adults would be seeking to complete an undergraduate degree, and that number has been revised to 12 million. The latest prevailing statistic is that 43% of undergraduate students in the U.S. today are 25 years of age or older. As the Baby Boom generation (I am one of those) contemplates retirement, we do not have a sufficient number of degreed people behind them to take their place, so the prevalence of adult degree programs should be with us for quite some time.

However, while teaching economics and business courses for years, I confess to a personal frustration with finding an economics textbook appropriate for adult students. Most economic texts, while quite excellent, are "overkill" for adult students; such textbooks were written for future economists or students pursuing an economics major in their undergraduate degree. Older students typically are pursuing some sort of "business management" degree that requires a course in economics, so these students want a book that will give them the basic principles and vocabulary to have a solid foundation. They want to participate in staff meeting discussions, get in line for a promotion, better plan their own employment careers, and become better informed when casting a ballot in a political election. After repeatedly apologizing to my students over the years, their suggestion that I write an appropriate book finally took root.

Economic Fundamentals for Adults is a meat and potatoes, "Reader's Digest" version of the normal encyclopedic economics primer. Again, such comprehensive textbooks have their place, but not so much with older students who just want to understand the basics. So, the volume has but 14 chapters; chapters 1-12 offer the no fluff approach to the basic economics concepts that a student out in the workplace should know, including why an awareness of economics is important, how supply and demand are center stage, how businesses form, why price elasticity matters, and how fiscal and money policy are used to combat inflation and unemployment. Chapter 13 seeks to provide an explanation regarding the causes of our country's financial crisis in 2008, and Chapter 14 seeks to prompt students to care about public policy issues by highlighting one (America's growing income gap).

Hence, I believe that this textbook is an appropriate, excellent volume for an economics course in an accelerated degree program for adult students. Indeed, a suggested course layout for an 8 week course is included, but one may of course tailor this foundational information to fits one's own needs.

And, being mindful of adult students that have other budget priorities, I sought to write a textbook that was reasonably easy on the wallet/pocketbook.

Lastly, this was a major undertaking that took a couple of years to complete; and, I could not have done it without the timely assistance of three parties. Please indulge me a moment.

First, while I trust I know economics, I know I do not know technology. I relied heavily on the assistance of Ms. Sharon DeVary who tirelessly labors as an instructional designer, online course resource, and technology professor in Palm Beach Atlantic University's Center for Teaching Excellence/Office of Online Learning. Sharon is completing her doctorate in technology and distance learning, and granted me hours upon hours of help preparing tables, graphs, and other special data presentations. (How can one write an economics text without tables and graphs?) Her own personal observations were also invaluable.

Second, I have enjoyed the good fortune of keeping in touch with many former adult students, so I unashamedly used them as a "focus group" to solicit feedback as chapters were written. These 25-30 adult students provided several meaningful observations and suggestions, and adjustments were made accordingly.

Third, my wife was a superior gage of my energy level. She was patient when I needed her to give me time to finish another thought, and she was inspirational when I wandered away from my focus. She watched my ebbs and flows of emotion and enthusiasm, and she seemed to know what to say to get me evened out.

And, may I give a special thanks to my publisher for giving me a chance.

TABLE OF CONTENTS

CHAPTER 13:

CHAPTER 14:

CHAPTER 01

WHO CARES ABOUT ECONOMICS?

Students often complain that economics is either boring or too hard, and I wish I had a quarter for every time one of my students sought to avoid taking the course, asserting that economics was not relevant to his life. Nothing could be farther from the truth, and those quarters would have bought me a new TV. (Maybe not a flat screen, but a nice little TV.)

While they might not realize it when they first enter the classroom, students have been living with the consequences, both good and bad, of economic trends and cycles all their lives. My guess is that most don't pay too much attention to economic principles until they feel a direct impact on their wallet or pocketbook, and I suspect those two instances regard employment and affording necessities. So, let's talk about those for a minute.

Every spring there are "a zillion" media stories regarding the prospects for employment. The nation's high school and college students do pay attention to these stories. An ill-equipped student may have difficulty securing employment at a local fast food restaurant (for the high schooler) or a nearby engineering firm (for the university graduate). The diligent, articulate, and high GPA student may have an easier time securing an appropriate position at a grocery store, bank, or non-profit agency. But the general stability and amount of growth in the economy is what creates the environment for all job seekers. During periods of "expansion", people will tend to feel better about their circumstances and spend more of their incomes on goods and services. That increase in "demand" will typically require employers to hire more

—

employees. Hence, job opportunities for existing workers (who seek a better job) as well as for new workers will be more plentiful. Conversely, during periods of "contraction" or even slow growth, many consumers are more cautious in their spending. Therefore, employers may need fewer employees. Job opportunities then contract, too. So, while education to acquire increased knowledge and/or skills is certainly a solid strategy, some years are better than others for graduates.

Besides securing a job, economics can have a significant impact on maintaining a job. One of the last headlines anyone wants to see is "XYZ Corporation Plans to Lay Off 1,000 Employees." Such a development may be due to a general decline in the economy, a financial crisis, or some problems that XYZ Corporation may be specifically experiencing, but the news will seriously affect the "consumer confidence" level of at least the residents of that town, if not that region, and perhaps beyond. And, what happens to the spending of those 1,000 employees who will soon be out of a job? Won't those families tighten their belts? And, what happens to the sales levels of the local restaurants, clothing stores, hardware stores, movie theatres, and so on? Ultimately, the level of demand for all sorts of items in that area will decrease, and so the employees at other companies in town will begin to worry that their employer may need to lay off a few employees. Will they lose their job? So, if they are concerned about the security of their future income, what are they likely to do? They will tighten their belts, too. Now, the declining customer demand just declined some more.

So, you see the downward spiral in employment, income security, and consumer confidence that can occur when layoffs become widely known? You can lose your job even though you did nothing wrong. Either a contracting economy, in general, or a serious mistake at a big company can "trickle down" to threaten most anyone's livelihood.

*Economics:
the process
of making
choices to
use scarce
resources.*

So, is economics boring? I shouldn't think so.

Or, how about another direct financial impact: rising prices of necessities. When food prices rise, people need to cut back their lifestyles and habits. People may eat out less often, or eating at fast food restaurants, rather than more expensive, sit-down restaurants. Some food items may be cut out of the family budget altogether.

And, what happens to families when the price of renting an apartment rises faster than the family income? What about renters who wish to buy a home, but mortgage interest rates increase? Or, just when they are ready to buy, there is a general "boom" of rising prices in the real estate market, and it becomes what is known as a "seller's market," rather than a "buyer's" market , which occurs when there are too many homes on the market?

And, some consider car transportation a necessity (especially if one lives rather far away from the workplace), so rising gas prices have significantly influenced family budgets and lifestyles. When all is said and done, economics is about making choices, and perhaps no single development has caused Americans to learn that lesson more than the escalating gas prices in 2007 and 2008, as well as what is now called "The Great Recession of 2008." People pondered whether to drive, where to drive, and what to drive, and a new round of discussions and political debates began regarding alternative fuels and long term energy policies. Many people lost their homes, because they lost their jobs, and could no longer afford to pay the mortgage on their home.

Again, was such an intrusion of economics into our lives boring? I don't think so.

Hence, economics directly, or indirectly, affects our daily lives. We may or may not understand how it impacts us – that's why you are taking this foundations course – or we may understand the likely impact, but disagree on the proposed solutions. (Welcome to politics, whether in the family, the workplace, or the government.) But, if you want to be able to make better, more informed choices about how to direct your life or the "life" of the nation, you will want to gain a working knowledge of economics and its concepts.

WHAT IS ECONOMICS?

If you learn nothing else, economics is about making choices. To be more specific, **economics is the process any group of people uses to make choices about how to use scarce resources.** The group of people could be as large as a country, i.e. a society, or it could be as small as a family, but an important ingredient in the process is the resolution of competing interests and priorities. While some resources can be replenished (e.g. trees), the world does not enjoy an unlimited supply of natural resources, and so there will be differences among members of a family or citizens of a nation on how scarce resources should be utilized to make products and services to satisfy various needs.

So, what are the two key terms in that definition? **Scarcity** and **choice**, of course. Economics regards how choices will be made, and choices are made necessary because resources are scarce. As economists are fond of saying, human "wants" are limitless, so even ample resources are not sufficient to meet everyone's desires; choices will be required.

Just what sorts of choices are we talking about? Observations of everyday life tell us that people prefer different sizes and styles of cars, different sizes and styles of shoes, and, depending upon geographical location, different types of clothes, let alone styles and sizes. Since a nation has only a certain amount of steel, glass, rubber, leather, cloth, and so on available at any given point in time, decisions will be required to earmark specific percentages of a limited supply of resources to make the various items that consumers desire.

Scarcity: when consumer demand exceeds available resources.

Choices: when limited resources force a prioritization of consumer demand.

Perhaps an even simpler explanation demonstrates how one uses time. Suppose you are coming home from work and you want to decide how to spend your evening hours before going to sleep for the night. After fixing some dinner, you realize you have four hours, from 7:00 pm to 11:00 pm, to accomplish your "wants and needs." So, what are your options? Like many Americans, you can slide into your favorite easy chair and watch television for the 4 hours. Or, you could snuggle beneath your most comfortable blanket and read some more of that mystery novel you started a few days ago. Or, you could get some shopping done that you have been putting off. Or, you could catch up on paying bills, return phone calls from friends or family, or do the laundry that has been piling up. Or, if you wanted to get a head start, you could read the first couple of chapters in the textbook for your college class that meets 3 nights from now.

Or, of course, you can split up the resource (time) into smaller units and handle 2-3 of the options you contemplated.

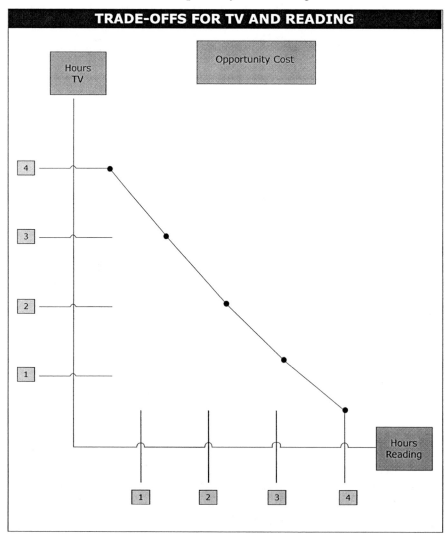

TRADE-OFFS FOR TV AND READING

Hours TV

Opportunity Cost

4

3

2

1

Hours Reading

1   2   3   4

But, why do you need to make any choice(s) at all? Why not do it all? The answer, of course, is that there is only so much time available. You probably can't handle all of the options within the limited supply of time (4 hours). How do you ultimately choose how to spend your time? Like most folks, you will prioritize your time; since this 4 hours is quite limited, you will decide which of the options can wait (until tomorrow night's 4 hours, for example) and which must be addressed now. Economists have a special concept when faced with such decisions: Opportunity Cost. The diagram on the next page illustrates the tradeoffs between any two of the options under consideration. (We'll pick TV and reading the textbook, but the concept depicted by the diagram is equally valid for any two options.)

Opportunity Cost: the value of the next best option.

Since there is only so much of the resource in question (4 hours of time), you need to make (a) choice(s) about how to spend it: i.e. spend all 4 hours reading your textbook (my recommendation) or any of the other options, or spend 3 hours reading and 1 hour shopping, or 2 hours watching television and 2 hours on chores, or 2 hours shopping and 1 hour reading and 1 hour watching TV, or …..As I trust you now see, the limited supply of the resource forces you to make choices about how that resource is used. This same "need to choose" is true for any other resource you can ponder.

SO, WHAT PRACTICAL BENEFITS CAN I GET?

1 Workplace applications:

This textbook was written specifically for adult students, so I suggest there are more benefits than what the traditional student typically acquires. First, since many "older" adults pursue a degree to help equip them for better employment, economics is one course that should come in quite handy when engaged in discussions at staff meetings, power lunches, or hallway water coolers. Part of enhancing one's professional image is being able to participate knowledgeably in conversations that affect the profitability and future of the firm. If the issue is a new direction for the organization, you will be better prepared to interact on a series of related economics subjects such as consumer sovereignty and market structure. If the question is whether to raise or lower your company's prices, you can evaluate your customer's marginal utility and re-assess your product's price elasticity. And, if the corporation wants to raise more funds, you can help consider the pros and cons of selling bonds versus paying interest on a bank loan. Hence, a general awareness of various economic concepts and principles should enable one to meaningfully engage in organizational problem solving.

2 Voting decisions:

Because economics is about making choices, power is inherently involved. And, power means politics, so sooner or later, an economics concern, especially a controversial one, leads to political debate. Indeed, most of the nation's "hot topic" public policy issues are power struggles over national priorities and acceptable strategies.

For example, recall Opportunity Cost (when choosing between reading and TV)? Another application of that "trade-off" principle occurs when a country must decide whether to devote resources to "war time" or "peace time," because every ton of steel used to make a tank is a ton that cannot be used to make a forklift or a bridge. Or, while Americans can indeed be very generous people, every dollar that is given to a charity that feeds hungry children in Africa or India is a dollar that cannot be also given to a charity that feeds hungry children in downtown Miami or Seattle. Should the U.S. offer more aid abroad, or does charity begin at home? We must make choices even when "doing good." Which priority do you prefer? Why?

Or, consider an actual public policy controversy that has troubled the United States for quite some time: the U.S. still does not seem to be able to decide what to do about our rising population of illegal immigrants. While the issue is now rather complicated, the original controversy pitted law versus economics; that is, millions of individuals crossed our borders and never bothered to become a legal citizens. Hence, they broke the law and, so far, are getting away with it. How come we are not rounding them up and either putting them in jail or deporting them? First, detecting them isn't easy, and the burden would most likely fall on employers who hire illegal immigrants: hospitals, schools, and social service agencies. Second, jailing and/or deporting (now) 10 million people will be expensive (and recall that opportunity cost says that every dollar spent on jailing/deporting is a dollar not available for another purpose such as education or health care or national defense). Third, and this is probably the major reason, many of the immigrants are willing to work for wages that are lower than what would need to be paid to Americans already in the country. Hence, consumers benefit by getting lower prices for a variety of goods.

Then, that issue causes us to think about layoffs and outsourcing due to global competition. If certain jobs weren't being done by illegal immigrants, the employers might simply ship the work overseas to foreign workers who are willing to provide their labor at wage rates lower than American workers. Has the U.S. standard of living essentially peaked until the underdeveloped countries catch up?

For another example, perhaps the biggest domestic controversy in this decade is the future of health care in America?. Besides escalating prices for all sorts of medical care, we have a rising percentage of citizens, mostly children, who have no health coverage. A growing number of American families are part of what we are labeling as "the working poor", which means they make enough money to be ineligible for Medicaid or other health insurance programs, but they don't make enough money to be able to afford a private health insurance plan.

Lastly, the economic issue that neither political party wants to discuss much is the increasing gap between the "haves" and the "have-nots." The only people in the U.S. whose incomes have risen in the last 20 years is the upper 1/5th of the population; wages have stagnated for the middle and lower classes. So, while the rich have gotten richer, the rest have been treading water, or even doing worse.

Now, politicians of both major political parties, especially candidates running for office, have a lot to say about most of those economic issues, and they typically propose a "three point plan" to resolve the public policy controversies. To be fair, candidates can't provide detailed plans on the campaign trail, but you can better assess the viability of those plans because of your awareness of economic concepts and principles. And, more importantly, your knowledge of economics should also give you insight into the implications and consequences of those political proposals.

So, this course will help you be a more informed voter. Some of you tend to vote Republican, others tend to vote Democratic, and many are Independents; regardless of your tendencies, I would hope that your ballots will be based upon your personal values plus sound (economic) information.

3 Personal financial decisions:

A third benefit concerns your personal financial decision-making. What career should you pursue? We have all been advised to "follow your heart" or "do what you're good at." That's fine, but what if there is no demand for that skill? Or, if making money is the only goal, which fields will be in demand for the foreseeable future?

What if you are contemplating a major purchase, e.g. a house? Economics will make you more knowledgeable about business cycles, interest, and taxes.

Speaking of taxes, there always seems to be a tax topic to consider. The cap on Social Security is being challenged; states are seeking to replace burdensome property taxes with sales taxes, and federal income tax reform is a never ending controversy; e.g. flat tax. And, for some Americans, the taxes they pay for Medicare and Social Security are higher than income tax withholding.

If you are an investor, should you invest in real estate or the stock market? Is an expanding or contracting economy good for stocks or bonds?

So, while this course is not about personal financial management, understanding principles and concepts of a dynamic economy will aid in your planning and family financial decision-making.

GENERAL HOMEWORK: Pay Attention to Current Events

One of the benefits of teaching and learning about economics is that relevant current events are so readily available. Pick most any day or week, and one is likely to read headlines like the following:

"Most Agree: Housing crunch isn't over yet"

"Leading indicators show a limping economy"

"Almost a third of CEO's to cut jobs"

"Poll: Fuel spike curbs vacations, dining out"

"Floods an economic catastrophe for Midwest"

"Dow drops 220 points, closes below 12,000"

Of course the headlines are not always this bleak, but these were representative of the economic developments in the summer of 2008, a time that triggered a government "stimulus package" rebate to taxpayers, gasoline prices that topped $4 a gallon for the first time in U.S. history, rising home foreclosures prompted by a sub-prime mortgage "tragedy", and rising unemployment. Government officials and economists argued about whether the country was officially in a recession, but there was little debate in middle income America that people were hurting.

As we noted earlier, students often lament that economics is either boring or too hard. Occasionally, some will assert that it is not relevant to their lives, but nothing could be farther from the truth – as the headlines above attest. Because of questionable lending practices (e.g. adjustable rate mortgages and interest only loans), families were being kicked out of homes they had lived in for a few years, rising crude oil prices caused "skyrocketing" gas prices that then reduced vacations, and therefore reduced service jobs. Natural disasters wiped out farms which then significantly increased food prices, and consumers became more cautious in their spending which caused layoffs in directly affected industries, which then dominoed into layoffs in other fields. Indeed, the expansion of technology around the world has created global competition that has all but eliminated job security from the American workplace., so at least one purpose of this introductory chapter is to convince you that economics is:

a) exciting and controversial, not boring

b) challenging, but understandable, and

c) highly practical and applicable

Economics hits us where we live, and current events prove it. I don't know what specific assignments your economics professors will assign in their courses, but I would strongly urge you to pay attention to the "business" headlines for the duration of the course. If you subscribe to a newspaper, be sure to look for national, state, or local stories, especially in the Sunday edition of your paper. If you prefer magazines such as U.S. News and World Report, Newsweek, or Time, you will find example after example of economics impacting our lives. And, if you prefer the Internet, consult your favorite "news" website every other day to keep up on the current events of the day/week. I happen to like MSNBC and CNN, but get into the habit of accessing whatever news website appeals to you; remain aware of the never ending developments in our economy that affect your life and mine.

Economics affects our wallets/pocketbooks, careers, and our country's standard of living. It doesn't get much more relevant than that.

MACROECONOMICS versus MICROECONOMICS

Macroeconomics: the "big picture" of economic topics such as growth, price levels, and employment.

One last topic we need to cover regards the two major broad categories of economics: macroeconomics and microeconomics. Indeed, in most colleges and universities, especially those that provide a liberal arts degree, there is one entire course devoted to each of the two categories. So, if you took a macroeconomics course, you would be studying the "big picture" of economics, i.e. the aggregates of economic forces. Macro means "broad" or "general", and typical macroeconomic subjects include employment, prices and inflation, money and banking, interest rates, and taxes.

Microeconomics: the subjects of economics dealing with individual firms and industries.

Micro, of course, means "small" or "specific", so microeconomics courses are focused on the individual consumer, the individual supplier, or a particular market. Typical micro-economic topics include what motivates a consumer to save or spend, how a business determines a price for its product/service, or where a person decides to work.

Since it is the goal of this textbook to provide a working knowledge of the fundamentals of economics, we will highlight key concepts from both categories into one "Readers' Digest" volume. I hope that will be the best of both worlds.

▶▶▎ *Chapter 1 Review*

Key Concepts:

1. Economics is relevant and practical.

   While sometimes "challenging" or "mysterious", economics is all about factors that impact our daily lives and personal standard of living. Employment, income, taxes, government programs, price levels, and global competition are some of the basic considerations that contribute to our personal well being.

2. Economics is defined as the process a group of people uses to make choices about using scarce resources.

   The world was created with limits on our resources, from land to oil to time. Since we, whether a family or a country, cannot have all that is wanted, choices must be made, and economics provides principles and theories about how the process of choosing should operate.

3. Opportunity Cost regards missed chances. Every choice that is selected also means that other options were not chosen, so the "cost" of the chosen option is the value of the next best alternative that was not pursued.

4. Increasing your understanding of economics will assist: 1) your employment and career, 2) political preferences, and 3) personal family finances.

5. Economics is comprised of two broad categories: macroeconomics and microeconomics.

Key terms:

economics, scarcity, choices, opportunity cost, macroeconomics, microeconomics

CHAPTER 02

BASIC QUESTIONS, SYSTEMS, & TOOLS

Chapter 1 sought to provide some incentives to pay closer attention to economics than perhaps you have done before. Economics affects our wallets or pocketbooks, our employment progress, and our standard of living. This chapter seeks to provide some basic concepts and tools that will serve as building blocks in future chapters. We will introduce the 3 basic economic questions, the 3 major economic systems, and some foundational tools and principles that will be useful for future concept applications.

3 BASIC QUESTIONS

Economics is about resource utilization, and there are three fundamental issues the resource allocation process addresses. To seek to clarify these questions, let me use a fictionalized bit of American history. Suppose we were part of the Pilgrim party that arrived on the New England shores to discover America. After expressing gratitude to God for a safe voyage, an exploration party needed to go ashore and scout out the landscape. Let's assume the party walked inland about 5 miles before realizing the sun would set before they could return back to the shoreline and the ship.

But, as far as they could see, there were trees everywhere. Hillside after hillside of trees. As the sun was sinking lower and lower towards the western horizon, these folks were faced with the first of our 3 basic economic queries: **what to produce and how many?** If you have any camping experience, the issue may be a similar one. You are surrounded by a natural resource, trees, but different members of the exploration party may have different needs. What are some of those likely needs? How about some shelter? Can trees be used to provide some shelter relatively quickly? Sure. Ever hear of a "lean-to"? Certainly, when the sun does go down, and with it the temperature, can our natural resource be used for heat? Of course – as long as you know how to build a camp fire. Or, perhaps some would prefer some makeshift bed so they are not sleeping on the ground. Or, some might wish to have a chair or stool on which to sit during the evening hours. At any rate, can you appreciate our initial issue? We have a resource and decisions to make: how many trees do we chop down? And to make what? "Tents"? Kindling and logs for a fire? Bed rafts? Stools?

That's the first question an economic system must address: what products (services) should be produced and how many of them?

However, just because I would like a lean-to or some firewood does not automatically materialize the shelter or the heat. Somebody needs to actually cut down the tree(s). Since chain saws are still a couple of hundred years in the future, I am going to be cold and/or wet if I don't know how to use an axe.

Or, if I am not handy with an axe, perhaps another member of the party is. Better yet, perhaps several of the team members can cut down a tree, so it is quite possible that the party will have at least a few who may be willing to "transform" the resource (tree) into a finished good (shelter, fire wood, stool, etc.). But, since it is unlikely that every member of the crew will be chopping down trees, the question is which one(s) will exert the actual effort to take axe in hand?

Thus, the second basic issue is **who will do the producing and how will they do it**? It is one question to determine what items are wanted/needed for production, but it is another to determine who is going to actually undertake the efforts to produce them. Indeed, what if every member of the scouting party could handle an axe: would it be a good idea for each person to focus on cutting down however many trees he thought he needed? We are, after all, in unchartered territory, so shouldn't at least some of our members be on the look out for attackers? (That notion, i.e. which task should a person specialize in regards another key economic concept, *Comparative Advantage*, and we will look more closely at that fundamental notion in chapter 2 as well.) Hence, once it can be decided what resources to use to make selected products, the next logical issue is some sort of strategy for determining who will be a "manufacturer."

So, our second issue is who will produce and how will they do it?

The third basic question is a matter of distribution. After it has been determined what products to produce, and then who produces them, the last issue is determining **who receives the finished products**? So, back to my exploration party. I want a lean-to and some firewood, but I am clumsy with an axe. Luckily, there are others in the group who are able and willing to chop down the necessary number of trees. But, while plenty of piles of firewood have been cut and bundled, how is it that I might get any? Wanting and acquiring are separate issues.

Hence, distribution is the third concern.

So, to recap, there are 3 fundamental questions that an economic system must address:

1) what to produce and how many?

2) who produces and how do they do it?

3) who receives what is produced?

How a group (family, nation, etc.) actually answers those questions is what economic systems is all about, and we turn to that topic next.

BASIC ECONOMIC SYSTEMS

Countries reflect different cultures that essentially reflect different customs, attitudes, and values, and these varying values are what lie behind the 3 major economic systems in the world today. Some economists are more comfortable with more modern descriptions, but I think the simpler approach is the use of the three "isms", that is, **capitalism**, **socialism**, and **communism**.

Capitalism: *an economic system that emphasizes individual decision-making.*

Capitalism, sometimes called a market system, is based upon a political philosophy that places a pre-eminence on individual decision-making. Most American students are familiar with the Declaration of Independence in which founding father, Thomas Jefferson, echoing the sentiments of John Locke and other thinkers, wrote that all men were entitled to "life, liberty, and the pursuit of happiness." That, of course, was news to the King of England, who led his citizens from a different philosophy and understanding of law. But, the point is simply this: who, according to the American revolutionists, is in the best position to decide what's best for you? You! Not King George, not future President Washington, and not even your father or mother (although you were welcome to defer to them if your sub-culture persuaded you to do so). The economic system that the United States of America adopted was a system that sought to allow millions of citizens to make their own decisions, including economic ones.

Laissez Faire: *An economic system that has very little, or no government involvement in economic affairs.*

A purely capitalistic economic system existed in the United States during its first 50 years or so. The U.S. practiced a "laissez faire" philosophy which meant that the government's involvement in the country's economic activities was next to nothing. Our economy was very much geared to a "survival of the fittest" approach, so apart from the creation of laws and a national defense, Americans were pretty much on their own.

Today, the United States government plays a larger role (some would say too large a role) in our economic activities, but America is still essentially a capitalistic, market-driven economy.

Therefore, capitalism is also sometimes referred to as a "free enterprise" system in which people are free to make their own judgments about what products they want, whether to start an entrepreneurial venture, and whether or not to acquire a product. The founder of capitalism is Adam Smith. Smith believed all parties (farmers, craftsmen, landowners, manufacturers, customers, and even the government) would get wealthier if each was allowed to freely (and legally) pursue his self-interest. Therefore, capitalism is an economic system that essentially accommodates man's natural tendency to be selfish, believing that one man's greed will be "checked" by another's.

Some examples of market economies include the United States, Canada, Germany, and Japan.

Communism: an economic system that emphasizes group decision making.

At the other end of the philosophical spectrum is communism. Instead of embracing individual decision-making, communism prefers to make group decisions. Based mostly on ideas of Karl Marx, who thought capitalism was primarily a mechanism for a few to take advantage of the many, communism places an emphasis on group decision-making, This approach is sometimes called a command economy, and the decision-making authority is based in the government or some central authority. Since there is a lot of dovetailing of politics and economics, most command/communistic economies occur in countries controlled by a political dictator. China, Cuba, North Korea, North Vietnam, and Libya are some common examples.

Socialism: an economic system that combines capitalistic and communistic priorities.

In the middle of these philosophical opposites is socialism, which is the economic system that the majority of countries in the world use. Socialism is essentially a "hybrid" of capitalism and communism, so both private enterprise and significant government control co-exist. Typically, the central government owns or controls some of the key industries such as communication or transportation, but otherwise encourages market forces to operate via individual decision-making. Most countries in Europe, South America, and Africa are socialistic.

In summary:

"Ism"	Modern Description	Philosophical Emphasis	Example Countries
Capitalism	market	individualism private ownership	United States, Japan, Canada, and Germany
Socialism	"command"	mixture of private and gov't ownership	England, France, Brazil, Egypt
Communism	command	group public ownership	China, North Korea, Cuba, Libya

At this point, it is important to cite a quick qualification, which is that no country is 100% capitalistic or communistic. Besides being labeled as capitalistic and a bastion of "free enterprise", the United States is also a "mixed economy", which means that America is mostly capitalistic, but now partially socialistic, too. For example, think of the term "*Social* Security." So are Canada, Germany, and Japan.

On the other hand, while China and Cuba are mostly communistic, each is opening to more and more to market-driven influences. So, no country is a "pure" representative of it's predominate label.

3 BASIC QUESTIONS and the U.S. ECONOMY

A logical, subsequent topic is how our economy then specifically addresses the 3 foundational issues. That is, if any economic system needs to resolve *what products are produced, who produces them, and then who gets them*, just how does capitalism go about providing the answers?

Consumer sovereignty is capitalism's response to the first basic issue. How does a market system decide what to produce? In capitalism, the consumer is "king." While surveys are often conducted to determine if there is sufficient interest, what economists call **demand**, consumers decide what products get produced by whether or not they buy items. Customers "vote with their feet" every time that walk out of a store empty handed, so businesses get significant clues about preferred products, product features, product colors, and so on from the millions of individual decisions consumers make when they buy or don't buy. Hence, in a market driven economy, resources are used to produce what consumers signal they want produced.

Who does the producing? Capitalism's answer is "free enterprise", that is, people are allowed to start a business to respond to perceived consumer demand. If you believe that there is room for another shoe store in your community, either because the current demand is greater than the current number of shoe stores (**supply**) can handle, or because you can provide shoes better than the existing suppliers, you are welcome to open a shoe store and begin marketing your shoes to the public.

Additionally, because parties are welcome to pursue an entrepreneurial venture (to sell shoes or any other product or service), a market-driven economy thrives on competition. While too many suppliers can waste resources as well as create struggles for the many suppliers, too few suppliers can stifle product invention or product innovation, as well as cost consumers more than is necessary. Hence, capitalism's market forces encourage a balance of the "right" number of suppliers by encouraging healthy competition. (How many is the right number is a subject in a later chapter when we talk about *market structures*.)

The third issue – who receives the finished goods? – can be answered in two words: price tag. Most every product marketed in the economic system has a price, so if you can afford to buy it, it's yours. Distribution in a market economy is not handled emotionally or necessarily ethically; who gets to consume finished goods is based on a simple, factual premise: if you can afford it, you can have it. Hence, in a capitalistic system, income is everything since the more income one has, the more purchase options one has.

A command (communistic) economic system uses a central government body to make such decisions. Planning boards are used to decide production levels, prices, distribution channels, and so on.

To reiterate, the diagram below summaries the major ingredients of a capitalistic system:

Basic Economic Question	Market Economy's Answer
1. What to produce and how many?	Consumer Sovereignty
2. Who produces and how?	Free Enterprise & Competition
3. Who receives?	Price Tag (affordability)

PRODUCTION POSSIBILTY FRONTIER

Opportunity Cost: the value of the next best option.

Recall the Opportunity Cost principle back in Chapter 1 (when choosing how to spend time between two options)? Because resources are not limitless, (in fact they are often scarce), choices must be made regarding which resources are used to achieve different desired results. While the Opportunity Cost concept could apply to any two resources, we applied the concept to the choices one must make when deciding how to use time. Given four hours in an evening, the diagram's diagonal line showed the possible options one would have between watching TV or reading a book.

Production Possibility Frontier: output potential and tradeoffs between options.

The diagram below is called The Production Possibilities Frontier and it is an extension of the Opportunity Cost concept. The Production Possibilities Frontier is sometimes called the Production Possibilities Curve, and the purpose of the concept is to illustrate the application of the Opportunity Cost to an entire economy. The PPF curve has three useful implications.

First, like the Opportunity Cost concept, a Production Possibility Frontier shows the trade-offs that a nation faces when deciding how to devote resources for production. As the hypothetical diagram illustrates below, a country could have several production combinations of, say farm products and manufactured goods; these various combinations points A, B, C, D, and E, depend upon what the country's citizens (consumers) want. As the diagram shows, the country could choose to devote all relevant resources to growing farm products and the production level would be the amount at point A. Or, at the other extreme, the country could opt to devote all relevant resources to manufactured goods, and the resulting volume of manufactured goods is shown as point E. But, if the country decided to produce some farm products and some manufactured products, points B, C, and D illustrate different combinations of production levels, depending upon how many resources are used for growing farm products and how many resources are utilized for manufactured items. Clearly, the more farm products are produced, the fewer manufactured goods will be produced. And, vice versa. Hence, the diagram is a picture of the trade-offs a country faces.

Second, besides showing the trade-offs between the product options, the PPF also depicts the maximum production potential for the economy if all resources are being utilized. The curve is the "frontier", i.e. the outside edge of maximum volume of production, and of course then any point "inside" the PPF represents a production combination that is a volume less than the economy's potential. Look at the diagram to cement your understanding:

Then, third, the PPF concept can be used to illustrate a very important goal of any economic system, economic growth. If the nation's economy is hitting on all cylinders, i.e. is fully utilizing its resources to

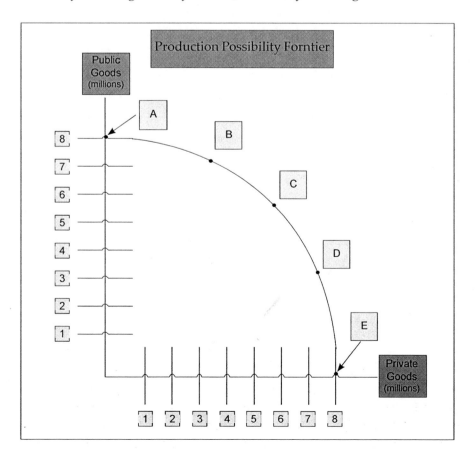

produce at volumes along the Production Possibilities Frontier curve, any growth in the economy means that the PPF has expanded to higher levels. See the diagram below. How can an economy grow? How can the PPF expand outward to the right? Answer: the economy acquires additional resources (e.g. new additions to the labor force) and/or uses its existing resources more efficiently (technological improvements). Conversely, how does an economy produce at a point inside the PPF Curve, i.e. produce at levels below its potential? Answer: resources are idle (unemployed labor), lost (land ruined due to natural disaster, e.g. floods) or used inefficiently. What about when corporations purposely make a resource scarce, so they can charge more money; e.g, de Beers and the diamond mines in South Africa? Or farmers in the U.S.? Will you address that?

ABSOLUTE AVANTAGE v COMPARATIVE ADVANTAGE

Absolute Advantage: the ability to out produce.

Comparative Advantage: the ability to produce at the lowest opportunity cost.

After reviewing the Production Possibilities Frontier and Opportunity Cost concepts, the logical question then becomes what products *should* a country produce? The PPF shows a country's potential as well as tradeoffs between options that different segments of the population might prefer, but given a country's (scarce) resources, are there products that a country makes well? That is, are there products/services that a country should focus on? Should the nation specialize?

Enter the economics principles of Absolute Advantage and Comparative Advantage. While we will discuss the 4 different types of resources in the next chapter, suffice it to say here that different countries will possess different quantities and qualities of those 4 kinds of resources, and, hence, not all countries will be good (efficient) at making all of the products they desire. Some products may require lots of land to grow or manufacture the wanted/needed items, and some countries either don't have sufficient amounts of land, or their land is too dry, too mountainous, too "swampy", too "frozen", etc. Some products may require a great deal of labor and the country's population is too small. Some products may require a great deal of expertise, but the country's education system cannot graduate enough citizens with the needed knowledge or skills. And, some products, while potentially quite profitable, require large investments in machinery and facilities, but many countries cannot afford to finance the necessary upfront expenses. So, for a variety of reasons, countries are not able to produce all of the products they want and need.

However, every country can and, therefore, should specialize in producing products where it has a Comparative Advantage. But, before we review Comparative Advantage, we need to quickly review Absolute Advantage.

Consider a small dental office. The practice has only two workers; the owner who is the dentist, and an employee who is the office manager - receptionist. The dentist performs the dental services, i.e. cleans teeth, fills cavities, and handles the more serious dental repairs. The office manager – receptionist answers the phone, makes appointments, greets patients, types needed documents, files records, files insurance claims, and sends bills to customers. Because the dentist has been educated and trained, he is far more capable of handling the dental services than the manager – receptionist. The dentist can be much more productive in providing dental care services. Because the dentist will be able to use fewer resources to accomplish the needed services, the dentist has an Absolute Advantage in performing dental services

Let's assume that the office manager – receptionist is young and has little job experience, so the dentist is actually a better typist, can file reports faster, is more professional on the phone, and so on. Hence, the dentist is actually more productive in the administrative duties than the office manager – receptionist. So, because the dentist uses fewer resources (less time, less paper, etc.) to accomplish clerical and management responsibilities, the dentist also has an Absolute Advantage in handling the administrative tasks.

So, should the dentist just do everything in the office? Of course not. Either the total number of patients served would need to be drastically reduced, or it wouldn't be possible for the dentist to handle the dental production and the administrative production. Hence, it would be better, meaning the office will be able to have higher production (see more patients) if each of the workers specialize.

While the dentist has an Absolute Advantage over the office manager-receptionist in both dental duties and administrative duties, each has a Comparative Advantage. The dentist has a Comparative Advantage in handling the dental tasks, while the office manager has a Comparative Advantage in handling the clerical and management responsibilities. While one has an Absolute Advantage when one uses fewer resources (than another potential producer) to produce the needed item, one has a Comparative Advantage when one has a lower opportunity cost than another potential producer.

▶▶| *Chapter 2 Review*

Key Concepts:

1. Economic systems are created to resolve 3 foundational economic questions:

    a. What to produce and how many

    b. Who produces and how

    c. Who receives the finished product/service

2. There are essentially 3 different economic systems:

    a. Capitalism (a market driven economy that emphasizes individual decision-making)

    b. Socialism (a system that purposefully combines capitalistic and communistic elements)

    c. Communism (a command economy that emphasizes group decision-making)

3. Socialism is used by a majority of countries in the world.

4. The U.S., a capitalistic economy, addresses the 4 foundational economic queries thusly:

    a. What to produce? => Consumer Sovereignty

    b. Who produces? => Free Enterprise

    c. Who receives? => Price Tag

5. The Production Possibility Frontier Curve shows a country's maximum output potential (if all resources are used) as well as the trade-offs in output possibilities as choices are made between alternative goods and services.

6. Absolute Advantage is the ability to produce a good or service with fewer resources than other producers.

7. Comparative Advantage is the ability to produce a good or service at a lower opportunity cost than other producers.

Key terms:

capitalism, laissez faire, socialism, communism, opportunity cost, production possibility frontier, absolute advantage, and comparative advantage.

CHAPTER

03

THE CIRCULAR FLOW
OF ACTIVITY

As of the start of 2012, the United States' Gross Domestic Product, typically abbreviated as GDP, was estimated at nearly $16 trillion. (That's trillion with a "t".) America's standard of living is the result of our volume of goods and services produced by businesses, and that volume is the result of actions taken by four key parties in what economists have called the economy's circular flow of activity.

WHO ARE the PLAYERS?

Most Americans enjoy an ever improving standard of living, (This is no longer true; author needs to look at minimum wage and wealth distribution over the last decade or so) usually measured by inventions to improve convenience, stimulate greater productivity, and create opportunities for (more) leisure. Few of us fail to appreciate the benefits of a refrigerator, a stove, a washing machine and dryer, central air conditioning, and indoor plumbing. Contemporary Americans take such products for granted (unless one travels abroad and faces more "primitive" provisions), and the United States' current standard of living is highlighted by flat screen televisions, cell phones, and wireless laptop computers. All of those inventions and innovations resulted from a generally healthy and steadily rising "flow" of resources, production, profits, and investments among the major parties who create and encourage interdependent exchange. Hence, an increasing standard of living is typically the result of an increasing flow of activity.

Party #1

Households: private citizens that own and sell resources.

Resources, whatever they may be, are initially owned by individual citizens. By tradition more than anything else, economists label this player in the circular flow as "households" or consumers. A household may indeed be a family of several people or the household may consist of just one individual, but the point worth making here is that resources are originally owned by private parties. The resources may be kept in the household for a long time (e.g. land or house), or they may sold quickly or at any time (e.g. labor), but the basic beginning point in a capitalistic economic system is that private ownership starts the flow.

Party #2

While it is quite possible for many individuals to provide for themselves, such independency and self-sufficiency evaporated more and more during the history of the United States. If you were handy and motivated, it was feasible to construct your own home, grow your own food, make your own clothes, develop your own energy source (e.g. water wheel, chopped wood, etc.), and walk, ride a horse, or build a wagon or buggy. But, if you were not sufficiently skilled, one needed to somehow acquire those products from a party that was able to produce them, i.e. a "business."

But businesses are just the "brainchild" of a founder (or group of founders) who needs to acquire resources in order to produce the item or service. Businesses either make a product from raw materials, whether a pizza, a box of cereal, or a car, or finished products are purchased "as is" to sell to the ultimate consumer. (For example, a retail shoe store in a mall buys boxes and boxes of manufactured shoes to then display on its shelves for sale to the eventual wearer.)

What are the resources that businesses buy or otherwise acquire from households? There are three: 1) land, 2) labor, and 3) and capital.

In order for businesses to make their products, provide their services, and/or pursue their various operations, they will need space on which to pursue their operations, whether a manufacturer, a wholesaler, or a retailer. Many manufacturers and wholesalers are big enough to own their own property; i.e., the business purchased the land from either the original landowner or a land developer, while most retailers do not own their store space; they pay rent to the party who actually owns the land (e.g. mall developer).

Land: natural resources

Labor: employees

Capital: borrowed money

Unless the founder and owner is the only worker, businesses need to acquire labor. And, how does a business acquire employees? It pays them some sort of compensation; i.e., wage. (We use a variety of terminology to describe the compensation strategies such as hourly wage, salary, piece work, and commission, but all of these equate to what economists mean when using the term "wage.")

What else do many businesses require to operate, perhaps especially so in the beginning? Money! The money, or "capital", may be provided by the founder, a relative, a bank, a venture capitalist, or whatever, but most enterprises require start-up funding as well as cash flow assistance from time to time. And, even if channeled through a bank or a venture capitalist firm, money originally was provided by individual private parties (households).

Why would anyone loan money to a business? Except for certain religious restrictions, (clarify)why would any party loan money to any other party? What's in it for the lender? The answer, of course, is interest. When you and I borrow money (unless from a very good friend), we are required to pay back the loaned amount plus interest.

So, just a quick recap: Businesses acquire needed resources from households (or other businesses who obtained the resource from a household way back in the beginning), and the households get a "reward" for selling the resource:

Resource	Reward
Land	Rent
Labor	Wage
Capital	Interest

Lastly, there is a fourth resource. This is a resource businesses need, but they don't buy it from households; they bring this element to the mix of land, labor, and capital. Businesses add "entrepreneurship," or risk-taking. Most any business in the cereal industry has access to the same basic resources of land, labor, and capital, but what differentiates cereal manufacturers from another are the management and vision they bring to the table. And, government statistics as well as surveys by chambers of commerce indicate that the major reason that businesses fail is "bad management." So, risk-taking is no small ingredient in an enterprise's success (or lack of it).

Why would an entrepreneur be willing to take the risk? What does any business seek when taking the time and making the effort to provide its product or service? Profit. Whether the firm sells office furniture or renders landscaping services, the goal is "making money," i.e. profit.

Hence, let's amend our previous list to:

Rent: payment for exclusive use during a specified period of time.

Wage: employee mpensation (i.e., salary, commission and wage).

Interest: payment to lender for borrowed funds.

Entrepreneurship: risk-taking citizens who start business ventures.

Profit:
*revenue
minus (-)
expenses*

Resource	Reward
Land	Rent
Labor	Wage
Capital	Interest
Risk-taking	Profit

Therefore, player #2 buys or acquires resources from player #1, adds some entrepreneurship, and provides a product or service in the marketplace. While we will need an entire chapter (our next chapter) to discuss the dynamics of businesses supplying (selling) products and consumers demanding (buying) products, the circular flow is based upon a successful cycle; i.e., customers tend to ultimately buy up the sellers' wares, the sellers pay wages to employees, rents to land owners, interest on any loans, bills to suppliers, and other financial obligations to any other creditors, and have some profit left over to repeat the cycle. And, repeat it, and repeat it, and repeat it. Sometimes employees get raises, sometimes businesses grow to the point of needing more land or more warehouses, and profits are mostly invested back into the business for possible expansion, but the basic cycle is what we have described; and, as we noted, the repeated flows were measured at about 16 trillion dollars at the start of 2012.

Party #3:

Government:
*federal,
state, and
local political
entities that
can also
produce
products and
services.*

But, private businesses are not the only providers of products and services. While many Americans believe that "the government that governs best is the government that governs the least," some government is necessary.

And, government is nothing more that elected representatives deciding what programs and services are needed to accomplish societal goals, i.e. safety and security, public health, family stability, personal mobility, environmental preservation, education, and so on.

Thus, government builds roads (or hires private companies to build them), creates a national defense system, provides means to monitor water and air and workplace hazards, establishes school districts, provides an income "safety net", and on and on. Citizens will forever argue about whether such services and programs should be provided, or what the size of those programs and services should be, but given that it is better to have 1 national army rather than 50 volunteer militias, or that Americans cannot be trusted to always compete fairly or manufacture products safely, some level of government will be necessary. Hence, government, along with private enterprise, will acquire resources to make products for public and private consumption.

Occasionally, government does sell its products and services. Consumers may need to pay for parking at a state or national park, citizens may need to pay for city water services, and government charges fees for all sorts of necessary services, e.g. driver's licenses and marriage licenses. But, the vast majority of government programs and services are paid for via taxes – all sorts of taxes. And, many of these tax strategies are controversial and worthy of public policy debate. But, for now, we are concerned with the Circular Flow of Activity, and it is sufficient to merely highlight that government (national, state, and local) plays a vital role in that flow. Indeed, government services and programs comprise about 22% of our country's GDP, or about $3.5 trillion.

Party #4:

Recall that after businesses acquire resources, they sell their products and services to various consumers wanting/needing their items. They pay employees wages, rents to land owners, interest to any lenders, and bills to any creditors, and they seek to make some profit when all is said and done. Hence, a variety of parties gain an income.

Financial Institutions: banks and other entities that receive saving deposits and make loans.

Hopefully, not all of the income is needed to cover expenses, so some households and businesses will opt to save a portion of that income. And, where will most parties save that excess income? Banks (and credit unions, and savings and loans, and mutual funds, and a host of other savings options) represent the final party in the circular flow. There really is only one function for money – to spend it – but there is some question when that spending will occur, i.e. right away or later. If the income won't be needed until "later", then most households and businesses deposit their savings with a financial institution that will protect their money and pay them some interest to boot. Of course, the reason the bank will pay interest to its depositors (as an incentive to be a depositor) is because it will, in turn, loan funds to borrowers who will pay interest to the bank. Banks are literally "interest middle men", paying interest to their depositors and receiving interest from their borrowers. And, of course, banks make money by charging their borrowers a higher interest rates than they pays to their depositors.

Gross Domestic Product (GDP): the current market value of the total final goods and services produced in the United States.

To summarize what we have laid out so far, see the diagram below.

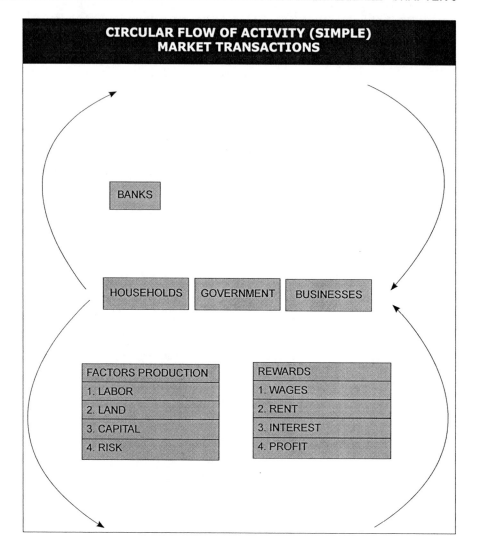

CIRCULAR FLOW OF ACTIVITY (SIMPLE) MARKET TRANSACTIONS

BANKS

HOUSEHOLDS | GOVERNMENT | BUSINESSES

FACTORS PRODUCTION	REWARDS
1. LABOR	1. WAGES
2. LAND	2. RENT
3. CAPITAL	3. INTEREST
4. RISK	4. PROFIT

Leakages and Injections

As we noted back in Chapter 1, the U.S. economy is a consumer-driven economy, and indeed customer purchasing comprises about 67% of America's Gross Domestic Product. To keep our employment from slipping, consumers need to keep consuming, and that means the circular flow needs to keep flowing around and around. (And this is exactly the problem in the U.S. right now; author should discuss effects of wealth distribution and a minimum wage with far less buying power than it had two decades ago)

The potential problem is that money can get "out" of the circular flow – and for some excellent reasons. But, when money gets out of the cycle, employment can be jeopardized, so we need a careful review of what happens when money flows are interrupted.

Leakages: taxes, savings, and imports

Earlier in this chapter, we noted that government is a major player in that flow of resources and finished products and services. Programs include Social Security, Medicare, Medicaid, welfare, food stamps, and unemployment benefits, while services range from national defense, police and fire protection, homeland security, and prisons to education, Veterans Administration, food inspection, mental health assistance, physical disability assistance, and driver's licenses. These programs and services require the same sorts of resources that private businesses require; i.e., locations, employees, supplies, equipment, and so forth. And, while some government programs and services are actually purchased by consumers (the government charges a fee), most programs and services are paid by consumers via taxes. All sorts of taxes. And, we'll discuss the types of taxes levels of government tend to use to pay for the programs and services they render to the public, but for now it is sufficient to note that government takes money from taxpayers (consumers) to pay for the buildings, staff, computers, office supplies, etc. Government may provide the program or service directly, or it may "hire" (contract with) a private company to provide the program or service. Either way, taxes are footing the bills.

Leakage: funds that drop out of the economy's circular flow.

But, here's the point worth noting: taxes are a leak to the circular flow. If money is taken from taxpayers, those sums then cannot be spent by consumers on the goods and services provided by private businesses. Hence, taxpayers would have less money in their paychecks to buy groceries, shoes, gasoline, and so on. And, less money to spend will mean less money spent, which can then mean less private production is needed, which in turn means fewer workers are needed. Employment is affected.

And, what if some taxpayers/consumers, with even less money to work with (due to taxes) wish to set some income aside for future needs? People save money for all sorts of purposes, including "emergencies", house renovations, family vacations, children's health issues, car repairs, and retirement, and these are certainly admirable and quite necessary. Furthermore, some are able to save more than others.

But, once again, a saved dollar is an unspent dollar; if I save $100 at my local bank, that $100 is then not spent on groceries, clothes, restaurants, birthday gifts, new appliances, and so on, While the saved money may be spent later, e.g. funds set aside for a vacation, the fact still is that the saved money hurts potential employment since producers will not need as many workers to produce the lower levels of goods and services due to the saved funds.

Hence, while savings is usually viewed as a positive development, what economists call the "Paradox of Thrift" reminds us that a good thing (saving more money) can cause a bad thing (less employment) if people save too much.

Injection: leaked funds that are put back into the economy's circular flow.

And, the third way money is leaked out of the circular flow is from the purchase of imported goods. International trade is both helpful and necessary, especially if American consumers wish to acquire a product that cannot be obtained from American producers. For instance, many Americans love a good cup of coffee in the morning, but since coffee beans are not grown in the U.S., the only way to have a cup of coffee each morning is to buy ground coffee from companies who grow and grind coffee beans. And, when we buy coffee beans that are grown in Central America or South America, those are funds that leak out of our circular flow.

To recap, money that is "out of the flow" is money that then cannot be spent on goods and services, and a reduction in the purchase of goods and services will translate into reduced production of goods and services; and reduced production will ultimately lead to reduced employment. To maintain employment levels, we need to maintain spending levels. Hence, the circular flow system needs to have leaked funds somehow injected back into the flow so as to help maintain the needed spending levels.

Injections: government spending, loans, and exports

Who taxes? Governments. The country's federal government, 50 state governments, and thousands of local (county, city, municipal, village, etc.) governments levy various types of taxes to generate revenue. But, government doesn't collect revenue just to acquire funds. Elected officials believe that constituents want provisions of programs and services, so the tax dollars are collected and then spent on those various programs and services. Sometimes, those governments hire employees to directly provide the service. Some workers are public sector employees who provide drivers' licenses, business incorporation, or medical care to veterans. Sometimes, government instead contracts with private sector organizations to collect garbage, provide mental health counseling to the disabled, facilitate adoption of special needs children, build roads, or build tanks. But, whether the program or service is rendered by a public servant or a private sector entity, government taxes are footing the bill. Thus, government spending "puts back" the money that was "taken out" by taxes. Government spending is an injection.

When saving money, people have two general strategies. They can hide it, or they can put the money in a coffee can or a suit case, depending upon how much is being saved. But, a more modern version of the coffee can approach is to save extra funds in a financial institution, e.g. bank (or savings and loan or credit union). Why? Because the financial institution provides a financial incentive to do so; it pays you some interest on your deposit. How can a bank afford to pay you interest for depositing your excess income with it? It takes your deposit, my deposit, and the sums from many other depositors to package a loan to a credit worthy borrower. The borrower may be a family wanting to take a vacation, a family wanting to remodel its home, a small business that needs to build a new warehouse, or a big business that wants to build a new branch location. Whatever. Financial institutions are literally "middle men" of money; they collect extra funds, i.e. deposits and re-route much of them back into circulation in the form of loans. Banks charge interest to the borrower, pay interest to its depositors, and keep the difference. (After paying its own administrative expenses, that's how banks earn a profit. The key is to find low risk borrowers.)

However, unlike government, who spends all of its taxes, banks can never loan out all of their deposits. If they did, what could happen the next time you visited your bank to make a withdrawal from your account? (If banks could loan 100% of their deposits, there might not be any money in the bank to give you a portion of your account when you wanted it. You wouldn't be a happy camper.) We will discuss the "legal reserve requirement" in a later chapter, but merely know at this point that loans (injections) cannot totally offset the leaked saving.

What was the third leakage? Yes, imports. When we buy products from a foreign party, our payment goes outside our "circular flow" to Canada, Mexico, China, Japan, India, and so on. That's not to say that international trade is bad; , however, if trade were one-sided; i.e., if we only bought products from foreign parties, we would soon have a problem. Of course, we also sell products to foreign parties, and those sales are called exports. When we export, we receive funds from the purchasers back into our circular flow. Buying and selling internationally takes us into the world of currency exchange (a discussion we don't need here), but suffice it to say that any country hopes to at least offset the value of its imports with the value of its exports. Presently, however, the U.S. balance of trade is negative, meaning we import more than we export.

To recap, America's Gross Domestic Product depends upon a healthy circular flow of activity, and we seek to balance leakages with injections. Leakages and injections can be thought of as a trio of offsets:

Leak	Injection
Savings	Loan
Taxes	Gov't Spending
Imports	Exports

And, then the total circular flow of activity diagram looks like:

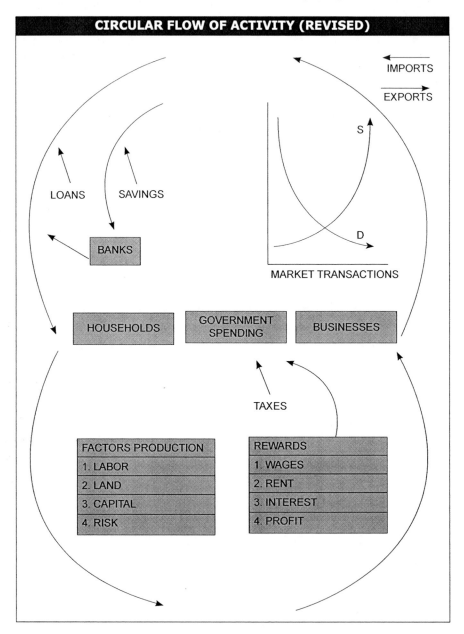

So, let's summarize. The American economy is a circular flow of activity primarily between private owners of resources and business entrepreneurs who seek to provide consumers with finished goods and services. Private parties sell their land (and other natural resources), labor, and even money to enterprises seeking to supply items that consumers want and need. After a cycle of making and selling, the flow of activity repeats itself over and over and over again.

The United States measures such activity with a concept called the Gross Domestic Product (GDP), and America's annual GDP is approximately $16 trillion as of this writing. As the U.S. economy has grown over the centuries, financial institutions, such as banks, and government have become two more significant players in the circular flow.

The amount of the economic activity pretty much determines the size of the labor force needed to sustain the level of GDP at any point in time, so it is important that money "leaked" from the flow is "injected" back into the flow. Hence, government spending offsets government taxes, exports seek to offset imports, and loans to borrowers help replenish funds lost to the circular flow as consumers save.

▶▶| *Chapter 3 Review*

Key concepts:

1. The country's economic activity is comprised of 4 interdependent parties:

    a. Households (consumers)
    b. Businesses
    c. Government
    d. Financial Institutions (banks, credit unions, et al)

2. Household activity (e.g. consumer spending) consists of approximately 67% of America's GDP; government spending consists of approximately 25% of the country's GDP: business spending (investment) consists of approximately 10% of the United States' GDP; international trade (imports and exports) consist of about -2% of the nation's GDP (that is, the U.S. has a negative trade balance at this time).

3. There are 4 major economic factors of production, and there are 4 corresponding compensations:

Factors of Production	Compensation
Land/natural resources	Rent
Labor	Wage
Capital (money)	Interest
Entrepreneurship (risk)	Profit

4. Money that "flows out" of the circular flow of activity is called a "leakage", and there are 3 ways that money leaks out:

    a. Savings
    b. Taxes
    c. Imports

5. Leakages are (mostly) offset by injections that include:

    a. Loans to borrowers
    b. Government spending
    c. Exports

6. GDP (Gross Domestic Product) is a measurement of the value of the country's economic transactions in any given year. Such transactions (circular flow of activity) have two sides: 1) expenses, and 2) income. That is to say, every transaction is an expense to one party and that same expense amount is income to another party. Thus, GDP can be the sum total of all of the expenses of those transactions, or it can also be the sum total of all of the incomes of those transactions.

    A somewhat more advanced way of seeing the importance of savings and investment in the economic circular flow can be indicated by a couple of mathematical expressions that view the GDP from the expense side and the income side:

    1) GDP = C + I + G + (X-M), where
        C represents consumer spending
        I represents business spending, i.e. investment
        G represents government spending
        X represents exports
        M represents imports
    2) GDP = DI + NT, where
        DI represents disposable income (net income)
        NT represents net taxes

    Since both of the expressions are equal to the same end result, namely GDP, we can expect them to be equal to one another, i.e.

    DI + NT = C + I + G + (X-M)

    Now let's just do some mathematical manipulations.

    First, DI represents net income, and there are two actions to take with income: spend it or save it. Consumer spending is already represented by the letter "C" (above), and savings is now represented by the letter "S".

    So, we can re-write the equation above as:

    C + S + NT = C + I + G + (X-M)

    Second, notice that "C" now appears on both sides of the equation, so its value will simply be offset or cancelled out when any final calculation is made. Hence, we can simply take that value out, and re-write the revised equation as:

$S + NT = I + G + (X-M)$

Third, we don't need to keep using the brackets for the international trade letters, so let's simplify to:

$S + NT = I + G + X - M$

Fourth, to "get rid of" any negative value, i.e. the $-M$, let's add a positive M to both sides of the equation thusly:

$S + NT + M = I + G + X - M + M$

And, of course the $-M$ and the M cancel each other out, so we are left with:

$S + NT + M = I + G + X$

But, now notice what we have. S represents savings, NT represents taxes, and M represents imports. They are all leakages. And, I represents business investment (loans), G represents government spending, and X represents exports. They are all injections.

Therefore, our GDP (our circular flow of activity) is a balance of leakages and injections. And, since, government spending should be approximately equal to taxes (yes, the federal government often runs deficits, i.e. spends more than it takes in, but in normal conditions, they are roughly equal), and since the value of our exports should approximate the amount of our imports, what we are really left with is:

$S = I$

Our economy works best when our country's savings levels match up with the needs of businesses to borrow funds to invest in America's production capacity.

Key terms:

households, business, government, financial institution, Gross Domestic Product, land, labor, capital, entrepreneurship, rent, wage, interest, profit, leakage, injection

CHAPTER 04

LEGAL FORMS OF BUSINESS ORGANIZATION

While it is true that free enterprise is energized by Consumer Sovereignty, (citizens turned customers send businesses signals regarding what products they are interested in purchasing), entrepreneurs are nearly equal in importance. Business owners are responsible for acquiring and shaping resources (land, labor, and capital) to facilitate raw resources into finished goods and services that can be consumed for basic needs or luxurious "wants." There was a time in our history when individuals were much more self-sufficient, and many provided their own food, shelter, clothing, and transportation. But, progressive developments in the last two centuries have created a much more sophisticated economy that values specialization (greater productivity), so we earn an income that enables us to then purchase our needs from others specializing in what we want. That variety of "specializations" is our millions of business entrepreneurs who comprise our free enterprise markets.

But, recall that the "reward" or "compensation" to entrepreneurs is profit; businesses are awarded profits for successfully taking risks. There are no guarantees that the business's products or services will be desired by consumers, or that the particular business's owners can effectively and efficiently collect and manage the needed resources to provide a competitive product or service. So, businesses take risks, and the life of the entrepreneur is hardly an easy one. Success may lessen the risk or ease some of the burdens of daily schedules or decision-making, but our economic system is designed to encourage and reward invention and innovation. Build a better mouse trap, as they say, and the capitalistic system will compensate you. Sometimes, quite abundantly.

But, let us turn our attention to the various legal forms of business formation. There are essentially four: 1) sole proprietorship, 2) partnership, 3) corporation, and 4) a hybrid of sole proprietorship and corporation. We need to look at each with a bit of detail.

TYPES of BUSINESS FORMATIONS:

Sole Proprietorship:

Sole Propri-etorship: a business ven-ture with 1

The vast majority of business ventures in the U.S. are sole proprietorships, businesses that are owned by only one person. Admittedly, there are millions of American ventures that are often called "mom and pop" businesses in which a couple operates the enterprise, but if such businesses are sole proprietorships, then only the husband or the wife is truly the owner; the other spouse is actually considered an employee. Additionally, most of us think of sole proprietorships as small businesses, but realize that legal type does not necessarily imply size of operation. Again, admittedly, the majority of sole proprietorships are small; indeed 90% of all businesses (which includes all legal types) are defined as small businesses, meaning they have 10 employees or fewer), so most sole proprietorships are small. But, there are also plenty of sole proprietorships that employ 25, 50, or 100 other people. Legal form does not automatically imply a specific size of operation.

Partnership:

Partnership: a business venture with 2 or more owners.

Partnerships, on the other hand, represent the smallest percentage of American businesses. (Why? The answer should become quite apparent in a few moments when we discuss the pros and cons of the various legal forms.) Partnerships are businesses that are started by 2 or more owners; some are family members or relatives, some are professional colleagues, and occasionally even "strangers" who barely know each other will band together to pursue profit. And notice that partnership need not mean pair, that is, a partnership regards two *or more* owners; many partnerships involve several owners, not just two.

Some of you may have heard of a special type of partnership called a Limited Partnership; actually, the correct term is Limited Partner. Every partnership, whether involving two or 200 must have what is called a General Partner, and most partnerships regard partners who are general partners. Each general partner is fully involved in the daily operations of the enterprise, participates equally in the big decisions that the business needs to make, and accepts full responsibility when "things go wrong."

A limited partner, however, is one who sees the business simply as an investment; he has no particular passion for the business' products or services, but he believes the venture is a sound risk from which to gain a financial return. So, typically, limited partners are individuals who contribute funds to the venture, but are not involved in the management of the business. And, if "things go wrong," their financial exposure is limited to the amount of their investment.

Regardless of the exact type, a partnership is formed when a partnership agreement is devised and signed by all concerned. Such agreements can be reasonably simple or they can be quite complicated, but the most common elements in such a contract regard roles, decision-making authority, profit share, and a process for adding, replacing, or deleting (a) partner(s). Like most business contracts, a partnership agreement should be created with legal care.

Corporation:

When we hear the word "corporation", most of us will think of big businesses like IBM, General Motors, or Coca Cola. And, indeed, many corporations are big, i.e. hundreds, if not thousands, of employees. But, again, legal form does not necessarily imply size. There are millions of small corporations, often a "family owned" business. In the now famous 1819 Supreme Court case (Dartmouth College), a corporation was defined as a separate entity apart from its owners. A corporation is "a legal person" that can enter into contracts, own property, sue or be sued, and pay taxes when owed.

Corpora-tion: a legal business form that is chartered by government.

Corporations are legal entities that must be chartered, i.e., approved for existence by a state, usually the one in which the business (or its headquarters) is located. Every state has a commerce division, and then a corporation bureau that receives needed documents from business owners seeking to incorporate (e.g. Articles of Incorporation) and approves (or disapproves) the application. It used to be that the incorporation process took a lot of time and money to pursue, and large, complicated operations still require the careful assistance of lawyers and other professionals, but many websites have now been created (started by law offices?) to assist many entrepreneurs with the incorporation paperwork at a much lower cost than historical levels. (Caveat emptor: let the buyer beware.)

Corporations are required to establish a board of directors that at least includes officers such as President, Vice-president, Treasurer, and Secretary. Some states allow an individual to hold more than 1 position, so a conventional corporation could be formed by as few as two people.

And, a corporation is authorized to sell stock (and bonds), although there is no requirement to do so. (Recall that "family-owned" corporation? Such corporations either don't sell any stock, or only sell it to people related to the owners. Hence it is "privately owned.")

Why would anyone want to take the time and expense to form a corporation? Hang on for just another minute or so; our review of the pros and cons will make it clear.

S Corporation:

S. Corporation: a hybrid that combines sole proprietorships and corporation features.

As long ago as 1959, the IRS created a hybrid legal business form for "the little guy" who wanted the simplicity of the sole proprietorship and the liability protection of the corporation; in sections 1361 – 1379 of Chapter 1of the IRS tax code, "sub-chapter S" allows a sole proprietorship to petition to become a corporation (of sorts) if the owner will agree to several restrictions. For reasons that are unclear, this hybrid was one of the best unintentionally kept "secrets" of the last few decades. If they knew about it, most sole proprietors would gladly shift to an S Corporation.

Limited Liability Corporation (LLC): a hybrid that combines sole proprietorships and corporation features.

While technically offered by states, the hybrid structure is sometimes better known as a "LLC", a limited liability corporation. Recall those websites mentioned in the paragraph regarding the traditional corporation? Those website authors, along with promotional efforts by most state commerce departments, plug the new strategy for accommodating the small business operator with big business exposure protection. The legal details may differ, but the concept is the same: create a hybrid of the traditional sole proprietorship and the traditional corporation.

PRO and CONS:

Sole Proprietorships:

Advantage(s):

Since sole proprietorships are so popular, there must a lot to like – and there is. One of the main reasons people start a business is because they had difficulties working under others when previously employed, so being the boss is a main consideration for such entrepreneurs. You can determine your own schedule (as well as the schedules of others), others must accommodate your management/leadership style (not the other way around; or so entrepreneurs think), and you don't have to answer to anybody – except maybe your accountant. You pretty much have the flexibility to make the business operate the way you wish.

Optimistically, another main reason to form a sole proprietorship concerns the ability to keep all of the profits. There is no requirement to share them with anyone else. Should the business be wildly successful, the gains wind up in your pocket and no one else's.

But, the truth is that the number one reason sole proprietorships are formed is that they are easy and cheap to form. Does an entrepreneur need anyone's approval to start a corporation? Unless it is an LLC, one needs no state authorization. And, a partnership of course requires the agreement of the other partner(s). Such steps require time and sometimes money. So, if you want to avoid the need for someone else's acceptance, the sole proprietorship form is the way to go. Minus s few local ordinance restrictions and the completion of some tax forms and other documents, a sole proprietor can wake up most any morning and start his/her own venture any time he/she wishes to do so,

Disadvantage(s):

Recall that entrepreneurialism entails risk, and statistics confirm that about half of all businesses that begin each year fail to see their first birthday. And, of all the businesses that start in any given year, only 20% make it to their 5th birthday. Hence, 4 out of every 5 businesses don't make it, and the majority of the reasons for the business failures regard "poor management."

And, the potential, serious disadvantage with business failures is what the law calls "unlimited liability" for sole proprietorships. That means that if the business is unable to pay the debts created by the business, the creditors may legally pursue the sole proprietor's personal assets to pay the business debts. Hence, if after liquidation, the business has no more funds to pay its outstanding obligations, the sole proprietor may need to pay the remaining business debts from his savings or be legally required to sell his car, house, or any other asset to settle the business obligation.

Unlimited Liability: a business owner's assets are not protected if business assets cannot pay business debts.

Partnership:

Advantage(s):

If partnership is not used much, are its pros few or insignificant? Not necessarily. The reason someone would create a partnership with another is because one believes the other has something rather essential to offer that will make the difference between success and failure. What are the common "extras" that a partner can bring?

One common "extra" is of course money. Many partnerships involve an individual with a solid product or service idea, but no money, and an investor who doesn't care whether the business sells shoes or lampshades. The key here is that one partner has the "smarts" to create the business operation, and another partner (or series of partners) provides the funding.

Another common combination is "personality and talent." While funding is not the issue, one partner is the "craftsman" who makes the product, while another partner is social and excellent with promotion and sales. One partner, Mr. Inside, works out of sight in the back, and the other partner is Mr. Outside, who works out front with the customers. Neither can do the other's job, and they realize that they need each other for a successful enterprise.

A third common rationale for a partnership is an increased array of product or service options. Medical, legal, and financial offices are the main examples of this circumstance. For example, rather than cause customers to visit multiple doctor offices, one doctor in this partnership specializes in cardiac issues, another doctor specializes in gastro-intestinal problems, while yet another doctor focuses on respiratory maladies. Or, similarly, one law office may have one partner who specializes in corporate law, another partner may focus on criminal law, another on probate law, and yet another on tax law.

In any event, the reason behind forming a partnership is that each partner believes he/she will be better able to compete and succeed by increasing the combination of resources that occurs when the partnership is formed.

Disadvantage(s):

Recall the major con for the sole proprietorship? It's baaack! If you thought suffering for the mistakes you alone made was bad enough, try suffering for the mistakes that one of your partners makes. That same "unlimited liability" applies to partnerships; that is, if the partnership does not have sufficient assets and funds to satisfy the debts of the business, then any and all of the partners can be held personally liable for those unpaid financial obligations. Thus, a partner can lose his house for the mistake his/her partner made. See why few businesses are partnerships?

Another potentially significant drawback can occur when a partner wishes to withdraw from the partnership, but wishes to sell his interest to another who will then replace the departing partner. Such a replacement often requires the approval of the other remaining partners. A departing partner may not be able to be replaced by just anyone.

And, if the partnership were but a pair, a partner who wishes out of the partnership may or may not be able to sell his interest: be bought out at an acceptable price by the remaining partner. Partnership agreements (business contracts) can get dicey.

Corporation:

Advantage:

The whole reason the law created corporations in the first place was to provide some financial protection for people's personal wealth. Many Americans question the ethics of such legislation, but the simple truth is that corporations were legislatively created to provide the benefit of "limited liability." Limited liability does not mean no liability; businesses still need to satisfy their financial obligations if at all possible, but should a corporation be unable to pay all of its debts, the owners' personal assets are protected. The corporation may go bankrupt, but the owners are not required to satisfy any unpaid bills from their own funds or possessions.

Limited Liability: a business owner's personal assets are protected if business assets cannot pay business debts.

So, why doesn't every entrepreneur want to incorporate and gain the limited liability protection? They do (or 99.9% do), but recall a business person cannot acquire the LLC just because he wants it; approval must be awarded by the state. Not all entrepreneurs are acceptable, and some don't want the expense or delay of the application process. And, some are unwilling to provide the information required in an application.

Disadvantage(s):

Whether a corporate form of business organization presents any meaningful disadvantages depends upon the needs and specific circumstances of the corporate owners. Because of a need for a board of directors, some would point to shared decision making. That may be real or cosmetic, depending upon the size and make-up of the board of directors.

Another disadvantage concerns what is commonly called "double taxation," that is, stockholders who earn dividends are paying taxes twice on the same money. Dividends are paid from corporate profits, after the corporation's profits are taxed, and then dividends are taxed again when received and reported on the individual's personal tax return. The same funds are taxed twice, once when owned by the corporation, and then once when owned by the stockholder. But, whether this is a serious drawback depends upon whether the corporation sells any stock; many don't.

Another disadvantage regards the possible expense and lengthy time to pursue an incorporation application. This can indeed be quite expensive and time-consuming for some corporations, but it need not be for all. The size of the business operation will likely determine the level of expense and amount of time it will take.

Hybrid (S Corporation/Sub-chapter S Corporation/ Limited Liability Corporation):

Advantage:

The benefit for an LLC or S Corporation is the same as for a traditional corporation, i.e. limited liability. Indeed, this is the reason for creating a corporate form, traditional or hybrid, in the first place. Small businesses were simply granted this same advantage by special government regulations.

Unlike the traditional corporation process, however, the time and expense to become a hybrid corporation is much less. That's why most sole proprietorships should pursue the LLC or Sub-chapter S process whenever possible.

Disadvantage:

The potential drawbacks to a hybrid corporation have to do with the legal restrictions imposed on the business operations, so whether these present any serious concerns just depends upon the business. But, for instance, one restriction limits the amount of sales the business can do with foreign parties; i.e., the intent of the government liability protections was to encourage domestic sales, not global ones. Or, another regulation (for the S Corporation) requires all board members to be American citizens, and another regulation (for the S Corporation) restricts the size of the board of directors. Again, whether any of these stipulations is an actual disadvantage depends upon on specific circumstances of the entrepreneur's business venture.

To summarize the pros and cons of the 4 major legal forms of business formation, see the matrix below:

Legal Structure	Advantage(s)	Disadvantage(s)
Sole Proprietorship	easy and cheap to form	unlimited liability
Partnership	combine needed resources	unlimited liability
Corporation	limited liability	double taxation; shared decision-making
Hybrid	limited liability	restrictions on business operations

TAXES and LAWSUITS:

One last discussion is needed to highlight two important considerations for the various legal forms of business organization, namely how taxes and lawsuits are handled.

The government taxes a business's profits, but only the corporation pays an actual business tax. Any profit that a sole proprietorship acquires becomes the income, indeed the wage/salary, of the sole proprietor, and thus the profits will be taxed on the sole proprietor's 1040 tax return. The sole proprietorship does not pay any tax on any business profits; the sole proprietor pays the tax.

Similarly, a partnership does not pay any taxes on its profits; the profits are distributed among the partners (sometimes equally, and sometimes not), and the individual partners will pay taxes on their portions when filing their individual 1040 tax returns.

However, since a corporation is "a legal person", a corporate business will indeed pay taxes on its profits. Income taxes are a business expense to this form of business.

Profits for a hybrid corporation are passed directly to the owners(s), so business profits are taxed when the owner(s) submit (a) 1040 tax return(s).

Lawsuits are handled in a parallel manner. If a customer is injured in a business that is a sole proprietorship, the customer does not sue the business, i.e. the sole proprietorship; the customer sues the sole proprietor. If the customer is injured in a partnership business, the customer sues the partners, not the partnership. But, if the customer is injured in a corporate business, the customer does indeed sue the business and not the owners.

Business structure is a legal issue, so different legal forms will create different consequences for taxation, lawsuits, stock share classifications, and other matters. Our purpose here is only to indicate that entrepreneurs and business owners have options to consider when starting a business venture.

▶▶| *Chapter 4 Review*

Key concepts:

1. Business ventures are legal entities that engage in economic operations with financial consequences.

2. The 4 basic types of legal organization are:

   a. Sole Proprietorship

   b. Partnership

   c. Corporation

   d. Hybrid (S Corporation or Limited Liability Corporation)

3. The major advantage of the Sole Proprietorship is that it is easy and inexpensive to form; the major disadvantage is that the owner faces unlimited liability.

4. The major advantage of the Partnership is a broader array of resources (e.g. skills and knowledge) that can mean a greater assortment of services to prospective customers; the major disadvantage is that each of the (general) partners faces unlimited liability.

5. The major advantage of the Corporation is that its owners enjoy limited liability; disadvantages include initial set-up expenses (e.g. by-laws and charters), shared decision-making (many corporations have influential boards of directors), and double taxation (if the corporation sells stock).

6. S Corporations/LLCs were created to provide the benefits of limited liability plus the ease of formation. There are legal restrictions that affect where sales may occur, who may be on the business' board of directors, and how many board members the business may have.

Key terms:

sole proprietorship, partnership, corporation, S Corporation, Limited Liability Corporation, unlimited liability, limited liability

CHAPTER

05

SUPPLY & DEMAND

Capitalism, one of the three major economic systems in the world, is sometimes referred to as a "market economy." A market economy is one that is characterized by hundreds, thousands, and even millions of individual parties making voluntary, independent judgments about how to utilize resources within their control. Markets are places where sellers of products and services "meet" would-be buyers of products and services. The mechanism that ultimately determines whether a transaction occurs is the price tag. Think of your favorite downtown main street, vending carts on street corners, suburban mall, "flea market" on the edge of town, or Internet website. All of them are "markets" where purchases of goods can be made. The marketplace may be as simple as a series of homemade booths at the county fair, or as sophisticated as a national franchise, or as "savvy" as the latest "dot-com" venture. (Think about this—is the dot-com example really a good one? Or, if you mention it, shouldn't you mention why it failed?) Each seeks to bring buyers and sellers together for potential transactions.

But, perhaps particularly in a capitalistic economic system, purchases are especially focused on prices. Several factors influence price levels, most notably the principles of Demand and Supply. Recall that, in capitalism, resource allocations are the result of three "forces:"

1) Consumer Sovereignty pretty much determines what products are produced;

2) Free enterprise pretty much determines who handles the producing,;

3) Affordability pretty much determines who receives the finished products

Since affordability is often based upon the price level, this chapter will introduce the principles and concepts that most affect the determination of a product's price, starting with two of economics' most bread and butter concepts: supply and demand.

LAW of DEMAND

Demand:
quantities
purchased
at different
prices.

For reasons that have somehow been lost to history, economists almost always label this material as "supply and demand", and yet teach the subject by beginning with demand. (So, why don't we embrace some consistency and label the material "Demand and Supply? I have no idea. I have apologized to my students for over two decades.) So, unwilling to break tradition, I will lead us first into the demand side of the discussion.

If you scratch an economist, he or she will no doubt quickly draw you a Demand Curve. (If you wish to take a peek, a typical Demand Curve is drawn a couple pages forward.) This curve is truly one of the foundational concepts in capitalistic economics, premised on logical, self-centered human behavior. The law of demand essentially says that consumers (demanders) make purchase decisions in direct opposition to price levels. In English, that means that consumers are more willing to purchase a product the lower the price becomes, while consumers are less willing to purchase a product the higher the price becomes. Such a "correlation" is called an inverse relationship. Think of the playground teeter-totter of your youth: as one child "came down", the other child "went up." And, vice versa. In the case of the Law of Demand, the two inversely related factors are price and quantity purchased (or quantity demanded).

Demand Schedule

The Demand Curve actually comes from data that is collected and put in a table such as the one shown below for, say cereal purchases:

Though the data on the table is straight-forward, let's just double check the inverse relationship at work. The schedule says if Kellogg's decides to sell cereal for $9.00 a box, 15 million boxes will be sold. If the price is reduced to $8.00 a box, Kellogg's can expect to see demand rise to 25 million boxes; if the price is lowered to $7.00 a box, more consumers will be willing to buy some cereal, and on and on. If Kellogg's decreased the price of its cereal to $1.00 a box, 130 million boxes would be demanded by hungry consumers.

And, of course, looking at the data in reverse would indicate that as the price of a box of cereal was increased and increased, consumers would demand (purchase) fewer and fewer boxes of cereal.

Table 5.1: Demand Schedule for Cereal

Price/Box	Quantity Demanded (in millions)
$9.00	15
$8.00	25
$7.00	35
$6.00	50
$5.00	65
$4.00	80
$3.00	95
$2.00	110
$1.00	130

This principle, of course, only follows logical, self-centered human behavior. As the price of a product declines, more of it will be consumed for a couple of reasons. First, as the price declines, additional consumers will buy the product who were not able or willing to buy it at the previous price level. Additionally, those who had been inclined to buy a box at a certain price level might be willing to subsequently buy two (or more) boxes as the price falls.

Similarly, as prices rise for a particular product, the consumer demand for that product will begin to drop off. And, again for two reasons: First, customers who were willing to buy the product at the lower price level stop purchasing the item, and, second, some customers who bought multiple boxes at certain price levels decreased their volume.

Hence, we have an inverse relationship: as the price goes up, the demand goes down; or, as the price goes down, the demand goes up. (This sounds counter to what American students are taught; what they hear is that when the demand is great, prices rise. When there is less demand, prices go down)

Demand Curve

Given the data in Demand Schedule (table), the graph below is really nothing more than a "connect the dots" diagram. The Curve is based on plotting the points that would occur from the data in the table, so, for example, one would plot a point on the curve by moving up the y axis to $9.00 and then over to the right (parallel to the x axis) to the quantity mark of 15 (million). The next point on the Curve would be plotted by moving down the y axis to $8.00 and then over to the right on the x axis to the quantity mark of 25 (million). Similar points would be plotted until all were located on the diagram. And, instead of looking

Demand Curve: a picture that illustrates what customers will buy at different prices.

at a Table that contained two columns of data, the Demand Curve shows in one picture that "inverse relationship" between consumer purchasing tendencies and price levels.

An example of our Demand Curve for cereal is shown below:

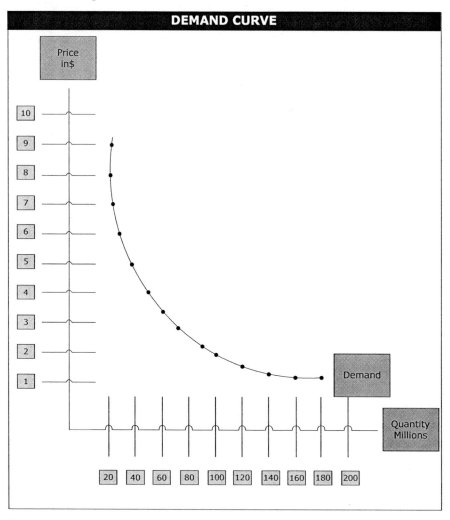

Graph 5.1

LAW of SUPPLY

Supply: quantities provided at different prices.

Now, stop thinking like a customer and think like a seller. While consumers are more likely to be interested in buying more goods the cheaper they are, what is the typical motivation of the producer? Just the opposite. The higher the price for which a product can be sold, the greater the quantity in which the supplier is willing to produce it. On the other hand, the lower the price for which the product can be sold, the less interest a producer will have in producing it.

Supply Schedule

Hence, a typical Supply Schedule table might look like this:

Table 5.2: Supply Schedule for Cereal

Price/Box	Quantity Supplied (in millions)
$9.00	100
$8.00	90
$7.00	85
$6.00	75
$5.00	65
$4.00	60
$3.00	45
$2.00	30
$1.00	10

Again, while the figures used for likely quantities to be supplied are fictitious, notice that the motivation for the sellers' reaction to changes in price levels is quite the opposite of the consumer's motivation. As prices rise, a seller is interested in supplying more, but as prices fall, the seller's interest also declines accordingly.

Supply Curve

Similar to the connect the dots strategy explained earlier, the Supply Curve is merely a pictorial summation of the data on a chart. The Supply Curve would look like this:

Supply Curve: a picture of what sellers will provide at different prices.

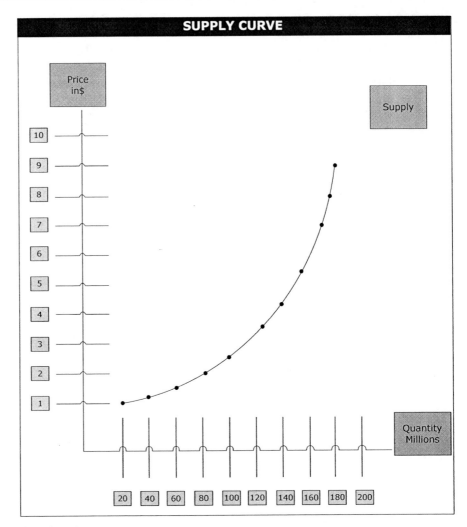

Graph 5.2

EQUILIBRIUM

Equilibrium: the price at which the quantity demanded is matched by the quantity supplied.

Separately, the Demand Curve and Supply Curve aren't all that helpful. We have two parties with contrary motivations. Interesting (sort of), but not all that useful. ☺

But, when we create a graph that unites the two curves, we highlight the foundational dynamic underpinning capitalism (or free market economics): equilibrium. Equilibrium means harmony, so look where harmony occurs in the graph below:

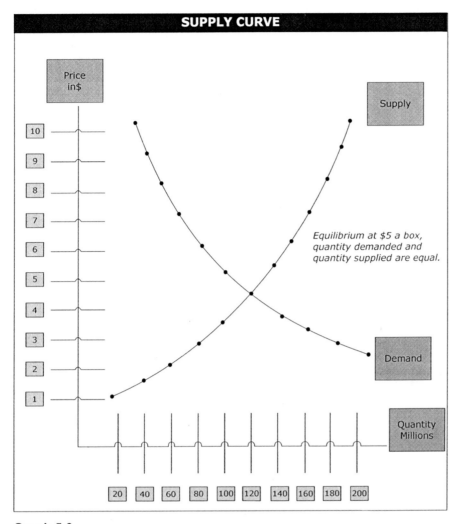

Graph 5.3

Notice the point where the two curves intersect. That's the Equilibrium Point, the price level at which both the consumer and the seller agree on the quantity to be purchased and to be supplied. That is, at the equilibrium price level, the quantity that buyers want to buy is exactly the same quantity that sellers want to sell. *Voila!* Both parties are happy.

Just to double check our understanding, take another look at the graph above. The equilibrium price appears to be $5.00. At a price of $5 a box, consumers are interested in purchasing 65 million boxes, and that's great because it so happens that at a price of $5 per box, Kellogg's is willing to supply 65 million boxes of product. Harmony. J

Surplus

Surplus:
a price causes
supply to be
greater than
demand.

But, of course, equilibrium doesn't always occur. There are no guarantees that sellers and customers will always wind up in agreement. Indeed, since equilibrium only occurs at a single price level, it is much more likely that the sellers will either over-supply or under-supply.

What happens when sellers believe the appropriate price level is higher than it turns out to be? That is, for example, what does the Supply and Demand Curve diagram indicate if the sellers supply quantities at an assumed equilibrium price level of $6.00 instead? The sellers would supply 75 million boxes at $6.00, but consumers would only be interested in purchasing 50 million boxes. That gap is called a surplus, and the graph below shows that gap with points A and B. Supply is greater than demand.

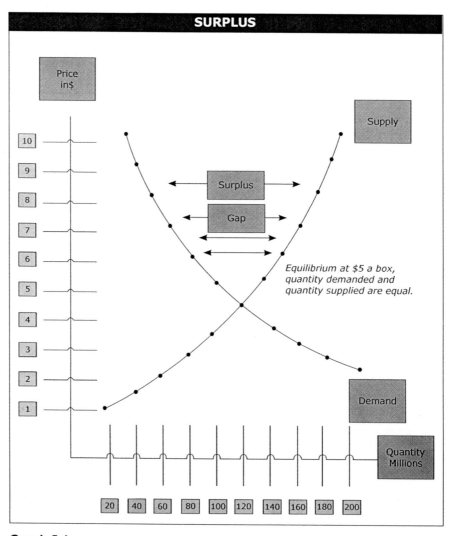

Graph 5.4

Notice what the gap would be if sellers thought the equilibrium price was $7.00? $8.00? Indeed, the farther away (above) we get from the true equilibrium price, the bigger the gap; i.e., the larger the surplus.

But, a surplus occurs at any price level higher than the equilibrium price.

Have you ever been shopping at a retail store and seen a big sign marked "Clearance" where a table or rack of items, often clothing, are collected in a corner of the store? The "Clearance" effort is nothing more than the store's confession that it guessed wrong and wound up with a surplus of those items – at its initial estimate of an assumed equilibrium price. What happened? At that price level, the store didn't have enough consumer interest: that is, the sellers and the buyers were not in agreement over the appropriate equilibrium price. Some consumers may have been willing to pay the seller's price, but not enough of them. The seller's "Clearance" strategy is an admission that it is trying to find a new equilibrium price to convince more consumers to buy the item.

So, by the way, what is the free market solution to a surplus situation? Lower the price till a new, acceptable price level is negotiated.

Shortage

Of course, sometimes sellers underestimate the quantities that buyers want to buy, and they don't produce enough. Christmastime can often create fads and unforeseen popularity of a new gizmo, or impending natural disasters (e.g. hurricanes) can create increased demands (for lumber, ATM cash, gasoline, etc.), or the first serious snowfall of the season causes a rush to get a new shovel or snowblower.

Shortage: a price causes demand to be greater than supply.

While most surpluses occur because sellers overestimate the equilibrium price and produce too much, shortages usually occur because of a "spike" in consumer demand. Hence, sellers supplied at what was presumed to be an appropriate price level, but the new equilibrium price level was driven upward by the unexpected jump in consumer demand.

Let's look again at the Supply and Demand Curve. What if the perceived price level was $4 (instead of $5.)? What does the graph tell us? At $4.00 a box, Kellogg's is only interested in supplying 60 million boxes, but because the price is so low, customers would hope to buy 80 million boxes. Another gap noted again by points A and B. But, this gap is a shortage; demand is greater than supply. And, similarly, the farther away (below) the true equilibrium price we get, the bigger the gap, i.e. the larger the shortage.

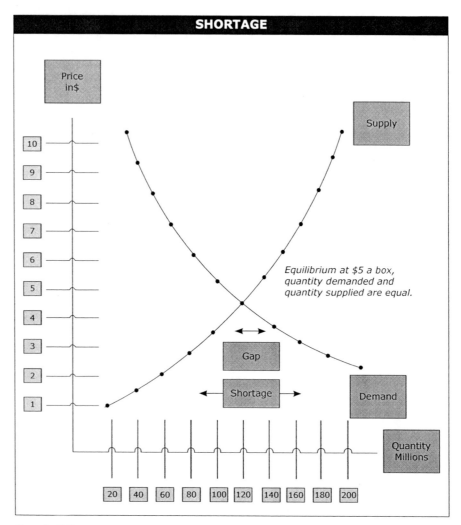

SHORTAGE

Graph 5.5

In reality, it would be unlikely that a shortage in cereal would be caused by an unforeseen spike in consumer desires for Frosted Flakes or Rice Crispies, but crop failures, for instance, could be the cause for reduced quantities made available by sellers. But, unexpected increases in demand do occur in lots of other types of products, so shortages do happen from time to time.

What is the free market remedy for a shortage situation? Think of an auction, perhaps the epitome of the shortage scenario. How many demanders are there? Several. How much is the supply? Often but a single item. (A painting or an antique). How is the true equilibrium price found? Whoever is willing to pay the highest price gets the item.

So, the solution in capitalism to resolving s shortage (in the short run) is raising the price. (Some retail stores, say at Christmas time, will instead maintain the initial, below equilibrium price to maintain goodwill, and restrict distribution via lottery or "first come, first serve" strategies.) And, the long term solution for a shortage, assuming the demand remains, is to produce more of the desired product.

Summarizing, consumer demand reacts to price levels, and consumers typically react in the opposite direction that price levels move. Sellers are also price sensitive, but their interest in supplying an item is typically correlated in the same direction that a price level moves. The two "warring" parties negotiate harmony at the equilibrium price level, often by trial and error (and consumers are notably fickle), and both surpluses and shortages can occur. If we wind up with too much of something, the free market remedy is a lower price; if we don't have enough of something, the usual solution is to raise the price until the excess demand drops its interest.

DEMAND and SUPPLY SHIFTS

Lastly, we previously drew demand and supply curves as if they were static, but in truth such curves "shift" around for a variety of reasons. And, these shifts will then change the quantities demanded or supplied at all price levels.

Demand Shifts

Recall that quantities desired by demanders (consumers) changed as the price levels moved "up" or "down" the demand curve. At $9.00 a box, consumers were interested in buying a very different quantity of cereal than if the price was but $5 or at $1.

But, an entire Demand Curve can shift "outward" or "inward" at all price levels for different reasons.

First, *expectations of the future* can change. What happens to most families when an economy sours? Newspapers tell of layoffs, stock market gyrations, or even corporate scandals. People begin to feel nervous about their own employment and whether they might get laid off. So, the natural tendency will be to reduce expenditures or even eliminate some altogether. Add millions of other Americans who are thinking along those same concerns, and the Demand Curve just "shifted" inward. See Graph 5.6a.

DEMAND "SHIFTS" INWARD

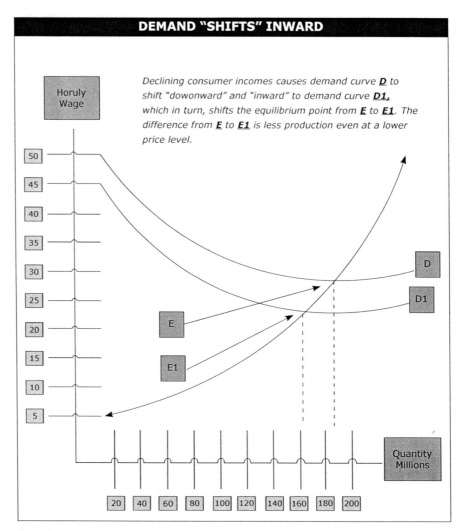

*Declining consumer incomes causes demand curve **D** to shift "dowonward" and "inward" to demand curve **D1**, which in turn, shifts the equilibrium point from **E** to **E1**. The difference from **E** to **E1** is less production even at a lower price level.*

Graph 5.6a

Second, *income levels* can change. If a full blown recession hits an economy, some folks will lose their jobs and those that still have jobs will be likely to curb their spending. On the other hand, for example, when gold was discovered in California in the mid 19th century, demand for all sorts of products dramatically increased since whole towns suddenly became wealthier.

Third, *tastes and preferences* refer to fads and/or long term consumer desires. Clothing items often reflect a new fashion "hit" for the season, but changes to smaller or hybrid car models reflect a long term preference change. This factor will usually cause a demand shift "outward".

DEMAND "SHIFTS" OUTWARD

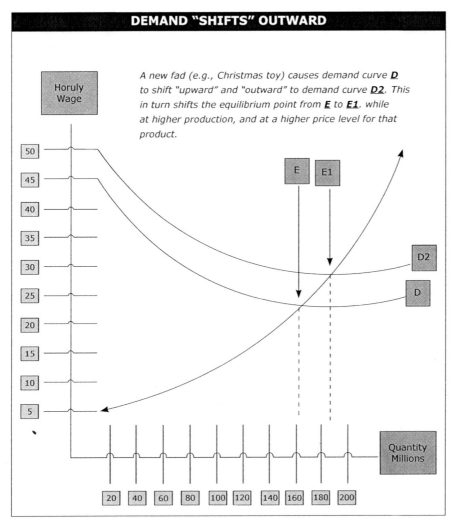

A new fad (e.g., Christmas toy) causes demand curve **D** to shift "upward" and "outward" to demand curve **D2**. This in turn shifts the equilibrium point from **E** to **E1**. while at higher production, and at a higher price level for that product.

Graph 5.6b

Fourth, *substitutes and complements* refer to related products. For instance, if the price of beef spikes up, the demand for hamburger may decline, but the demand for chicken may then receive a boost as shoppers substitute chicken for beef. And, since many people enjoy condiments like ketchup, mustard, and pickle relish on their hamburgers, a rise in summer beef prices may then also cause a decline in demand for the complementary condiment products.

Supply Shifts

Supply factors can change, too, which cause whole Supply Curves to shift "outward" or "inward."

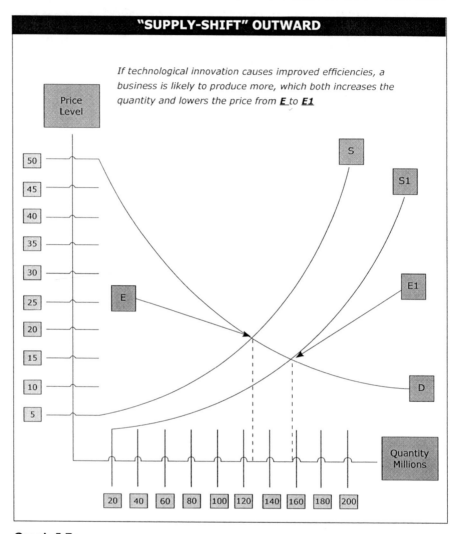

"SUPPLY-SHIFT" OUTWARD

*If technological innovation causes improved efficiencies, a business is likely to produce more, which both increases the quantity and lowers the price from **E** to **E1***

Graph 5.7a

"SUPPLY-SHIFT" INWARD

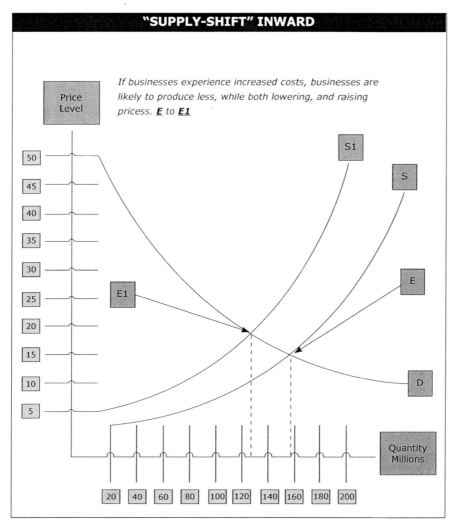

*If businesses experience increased costs, businesses are likely to produce less, while both lowering, and raising pricess. **E** to **E1***

Graph 5.7b

First, *cost of resources* has a significant influence on quantities supplied. If the price of raw materials increases or decreases, the resulting cost to make the item can alter a seller's willingness or ability to supply the finished goods.

Second, *technology* itself can have a major impact on the ability of a supplier to provide the finished good more efficiently, i.e. more economically.

While the "cost of resources" determinant usually causes a supply curve to shift inward (because most of the time the costs of resources increase rather than decrease), the usual consequence of technology innovations is an outward shift of the supply curve.

Third, *expectations of the future* will impact supplies at all price levels. Just as the anticipations and comfort levels of consumers can shift demands upward/outward during good times or downward/

inward during anxious times, such mindsets can equally occur in business/supplier thinking. If sellers come to believe that the future economic climate will be "sour", they can reduce production efforts accordingly at all price levels. Or they may come to believe that the future economic environment will increase, so they will respond with improved production levels at all price options.

To reiterate, the ever competing "determinants" of demand and supply are:

Causes for a Demand Curve Shift	Causes for a Supply Curve Shift
Costs of Complements/Supplements	Costs of raw materials/inventory
Tastes and preferences	Technological improvements
Expectations of Future	Expectations of Future
Income Growth/Decline of consumers	

CHAPTER SUMMARY

The concepts of Demand and Supply comprise the most foundational model of a free enterprise economic system. Adam Smith, the acclaimed founder of capitalism and a free market system, first used the phrase in his famous volume, *The Wealth of Nations* in 1776. The language is the essential cornerstone of an economy that allows resources to be allocated based upon millions and millions of individual, independent decisions by buyers and sellers. The basic supply and demand principles predict price changes as consumers send signals to sellers about their willingness to make purchases at various price level options, and sellers both plan and react accordingly. While surpluses and shortages can occur, a free moving price can increase or decrease as needed so as to ultimately create equilibrium where quantities "demanded" by buyers are matched by quantities "supplied" by sellers. Waste can develop when sellers use resources to oversupply consumer demand for items, but the American free enterprise system is actually quite efficient, in general, in utilizing and allocating resources to meet the needs and wants of American citizens. Prices rise and fall to reach equilibrium quite effectively, and usually rather quickly.

Lastly, there are a number of factors that contribute to the "shifting" levels of consumer demand and/or seller supplies which affect quantities bought and sold at all price options. Those factors, or *determinants*, can shift a curve outward (higher quantities) or inward (lower quantities), which then creates new equilibrium points.

▶▶| *Chapter 5 Review*

Key concepts:

1. Demand is the level of interest in products or services by consumers. Typically, the higher the price of the product or service, the lower the amount of interest there will be for the item. Conversely, as prices decline, consumption of the product or service usually rises.

2. Supply regards the amount of a good or service provided by a seller. Suppliers have just the opposite motivation as demanders (consumers); as prices increase, sellers are interested in supplying more of the item, and as prices decrease, sellers are interested in supplying less.

3. The price level at which the quantity wanted by consumers matches the quantity provided by suppliers is called equilibrium. Harmony exists because, at this specific price, the quantity demanded by consumers is matched by the quantity supplied by sellers.

4. A surplus occurs when the quantity of a good supplied by sellers exceeds the quantity desired by customers. A surplus usually occurs because the seller is seeking to sell at a price level higher than consumers are willing to pay.

5. A shortage occurs when the quantity of a good demanded by consumers exceeds the quantity supplied by sellers. A shortage occurs because the seller's price is too low, though many shortages occur because of an unanticipated spike in demand due to fad or weather developments.

6. The entire Demand Curve can "shift" inward or outward (at all price levels) due to changes in income levels, tastes and preferences, expectations about the future, and/or substitutes and complements.

7. The entire Supply Curve can "shift" inward or outward (at all price levels) due to changes in business costs, improvements in technology, and/or expectations about the future.

Key terms:

demand, supply, Demand Curve, Supply Curve, Demand Shift, Supply Shift, equilibrium, surplus, shortage

CHAPTER 06

MARGINAL UTILITY AND PRICE ELASTICITY

MARGINAL UTILITY

Have you ever seen or used a vending machine for newspapers? One can put in the required number of coins (usually quarters), then one can lift up a lid to access a pile of newspapers, and one can take a paper off the top of the pile. Actually, once the coins are inserted and the lid is open, there is nothing to stop a person from taking several papers, even the whole pile. Yet, the newspaper company isn't worried that will happen. Why not? The answer has to do with an economic concept called *marginal utility*.

Marginal: *extra or additional amount.*

When was the last time you enjoyed an all-you-can-eat buffet? I think my favorite is a local Chinese restaurant, but I'm sure there are all kinds of ethnic all-you-can-eat restaurant options. If, for one price (some are no doubt high, but most are reasonable), customers can eat as much as they want, why don't such restaurants quickly go out of business? The answer is, again, *marginal utility*.

Utility: *joy or satisfaction.*

The term *utility* in economics means level of pleasure, satisfaction, or joy, and marginal means extra amount or last amount. So, marginal utility refers to the amount of extra enjoyment one gains when experiencing an additional or extra consumption. Suppose it is summer time and you just came into the kitchen from working for a couple of hours outside in the hot sun. You are thirsty and look inside the refrigerator to consider something to drink; someone has made a pitcher

Marginal Utility: *additional pleasure gained from consuming 1 more of something.*

of lemonade. You grab a glass from a cupboard, pour some, and you thoroughly enjoy a glass of cold lemonade. But, while tasty, it was not thirst quenching, so you pour and enjoy a second glass of lemonade. And, indeed, the second glass did not quite quench your thirst, so you consume some lemonade for a third and final time.

But, here's the point. While you enjoyed each of the 3 glasses of lemonade, you did not (probably) enjoy each glass of lemonade with the same level of enjoyment. While glass #2 was pleasurable, the amount of satisfaction from consuming the second glass of lemonade, your marginal utility, was not as high as the level of satisfaction you got when consuming glass #1. Similarly, while the third glass of lemonade was also pleasurable, you no doubt took longer to drink it since, by then, your thirst was nearly quenched, so the amount of joy you got from the third consumption, the marginal utility, was lower than the level of pleasure from drinking glass #2. Each glass of lemonade brought joy, but the level of pleasure gained with each successive glass was lower and lower.

And, that's what the all-you-can-eat restaurant is counting on. The restaurant owner is expecting marginal utility to "kick in" and prevent you from never ending consumption; then he would go broke. But, after 2-3 plates of food, most people's marginal utility, levels of pleasure from additional consumption, will stop being positive. If they continue to consume, they will make themselves quite uncomfortable, if not sick. Marginal utility declines and declines down to almost zero – and most people don't want to risk a negative utility; i.e., becoming ill by eating too much.

And, why is the newspaper publisher not too worried that people will steal extra newspapers when the lid if lifted? Because the marginal utility of consuming (owning) a second newspaper is zero. If you have one copy of the newspaper, that you can read as many times as you wish, what greater amount of pleasure is there by having a second copy? None. So, taking more than one copy of the newspaper is rather pointless; newspaper publishers are banking on the economic concept of marginal utility.

For one last example, Universal Studios (near Orlando, FL) promoted a marketing gimmick that allowed patrons who bought a ticket to return to the attraction the following day for free. In essence, customers would pay for one day's amusements and get a second day for free. And, Universal Studios has almost no second day consumers. It sells plenty of tickets to customers, but very few return the next day. Why? Because, again, the marginal utility for consuming a second day of Universal Studios is zero for most people. While quite enjoyable, Universal Studios is not that large of a park. Unlike the much larger Disney World a customer can pretty much experience (consume) everything there is to see and do at Universal Studios in one day. A second consumption of Universal Studios, returning for day number two, won't generate much marginal utility (additional pleasure).

Recall from Chapter One that at its essence, economics is about making choices, and customers make choices "at the margin." Given limited resources of time and/or money, consumers make choices between options based upon real or perceived differences in levels of enjoyment that occur at different levels of consumption. Not only did our thirsty gardener have different levels of enjoyment for different consumptions (glasses) of lemonade, would the choice to drink lemonade still have been made if the gardener had the option of iced tea instead? Or his favorite soda? Choices become a bit more complex when we have options, each with its own differing levels of enjoyment.

Let's try an example. Assume you have $3.00 to spend, and you are using the drive-thru strategy of a local bakery. Assuming the following data regards the personal preferences of Mr. Jones, how would Mr. Jones spend his funds? What would he choose to buy?

The solution is a two-step process. The first step regards the "calculation" of each product's marginal utility for this consumer.

Consume	Beverages				Donuts					
	Coffee $1		Juice $1		Glazed $.50		Plain $.50		Fritter $1	
	TU	MU	TU	MU	TU	MU	TU	MU	TU	MU
1	15		10		6		5		8	
2	24		15		11		9		15	
3	27		17		13		12		21	
4	28		18		15		14		26	
5	27		15		16		15		20	
6	20		10		15		14		15	

Let's review what the chart indicates. In this case, the consumer has five items he could potentially purchase, two beverages and three donut options. And, there are two columns of data for each product alternative; the TU column regards the **total utility** that this consumer receives from consuming various amounts of an item, and the MU column regards the **marginal utility** that this consumer gains from drinking or eating various amounts of coffee, juice, or donuts. (Remember from earlier examples that marginal utility is all about how much satisfaction or pleasure one gets when consuming something, and then consuming some more of that same item.)

Clearly the data changes at different levels of consumption. For example, if this customer were to consume an initial cup of coffee, he would enjoy a **total** pleasure level of 15, but if he drank a second cup of coffee, his **total** amount of pleasure (for the two cups) increases to 24. If he opted to purchase and drink a third cup, his **total** pleasure would rise to 27, and so on. (Notice that if he were to drink a fourth cup, his **total** pleasure wouldn't increase much beyond the pleasure he had accumulated after the 3rd cup, and if he were to drink a 5th cup, the **total** level of accumulated pleasure would decline. (That last cup of coffee would not be pleasurable. It would leave a bad taste in his mouth, ("coffee-breath") make him sick or uncomfortable or otherwise cause a negative reaction.)

What are the indications if the customer instead drank juice? According to the chart, he would get a pleasure level of 10 for consuming the first bottle. If he drank juice again, the accumulated pleasure level, total utility, jumps to 15, a third consumption of juice would cause a total pleasure level of 17, and so on. Notice that, much like the pattern with the coffee option, that increased consumption of juice leads to a declining accumulation of pleasure in the higher levels of consumption.

If he opted to eat a donut instead, the level of pleasure for the first glazed donut would be 6, the first plain donut would be 5, or the first fritter would give the consumer a pleasure level of 8. The pleasure levels change if the consumer eats a second glazed donut, a plain donut, or a fritter to 11, 9, or 15, respectively. And, once again, if the consumer eats enough of the same item, the accumulated level of enjoyment, the total utility, starts to decrease at the higher consumption levels. (One gets "sick" of eating too much of something that previously was enjoyable.)

But, we aren't so much interested in the customer's total utility as we are his marginal utility. Hence, the blank column needs to be filled in. How do we do that? Quite simply, really. Look back to the columns regarding coffee. The chart indicates that if the consumer purchases and drinks an initial cup of coffee, the accumulated level of pleasure is 15. And, since he has only consumed 1 cup of coffee at that point, the marginal utility, i.e. the amount of enjoyment he gained for consuming an "extra" amount of something, is that same 15. But, should he consume a second cup of coffee, his total amount of pleasure is now 24, that is, the two cups have combined to increase his level of accumulated pleasure from 15 to 24. If the first cup caused an enjoyment level of 15, what amount of pleasure must the second cup have generated to reach a total of 24? That is, $15 + X = 24$? And, $X = ?$ ($X = 24 - 15$, or 9) The marginal utility, the amount of pleasure in the additional consumption, for cup #2 number two of coffee is nine. Nine is i.e. the difference between the total utility at that point minus the previous total utility.

Hence, if the consumer drinks a third cup of coffee, what is the level of pleasure he gets from just that third cup? What is the total utility at consumption level three? 27. What was the accumulated pleasure at the previous level of two? 24. So, the marginal utility of a 3rd cup of coffee is $27 - 24$, or three.

If he were to drink a 4th cup of coffee, the marginal utility for that 4th cup would be $28 - 27$, or one; the marginal utility for the 5th consumption of coffee would be $27 - 28 =$ minus one and the marginal utility for the 6th cup of coffee would be $20 - 27 =$ minus 7.

So, if we were to "calculate" the various marginal utility figures, i.e. fill in the blanks for the 5 MU columns of the prior chart, we would have the following:

Consume	Beverages				Donuts					
	Coffee $1		Juice $1		Glazed $.50		Plain $.50		Fritter $1	
	TU	MU	TU	MU	TU	MU	TU	MU	TU	MU
1	15	15	10	10	6	6	5	5	8	8
2	24	9	15	5	11	5	9	4	15	7
3	27	3	17	2	13	2	12	3	21	6
4	28	1	18	1	15	2	14	2	26	5
5	27	-1	15	-3	16	1	15	1	20	-6
6	20	-7	10	-5	15	-1	14	-1	15	-5

After determining the marginal utilities for the product options at the given consumption levels (6, in this situation), the second step in the solution process is to make comparisons of the marginal utility numbers between the product alternatives.

Notice that items cost either $1 or fifty cents, so while the customer has $3 to spend, it will be easiest to make 3 one-dollar decisions.

So, what could our customer purchase with his first dollar? He could purchase a cup of coffee, and consuming coffee for the first time would yield a marginal utility (amount of pleasure) of 15.

Or, he could instead use the $1 to purchase and consume some juice. According to the chart of data for this person, consuming juice for the first time would yield a marginal utility of 10.

Or, he could consume some donuts. If he spent his first $1 on glazed donuts, he could get 2 donuts (since they cost but $.50 each), and the marginal utility for 2 glazed donuts is 6 (glazed donut #1) + 5 (glazed donut #2), or 11.

If he purchased and consumed plain donuts, he would have a marginal utility level of 5 (plain donut #1) + 4 (plain donut #2), or 9.

Lastly, he could instead purchase a fritter, and the marginal utility for consuming a first fritter is 8.

Hence, among the purchase/consumption options, he could achieve levels of pleasure of:

a)   15 (a cup of coffee),

b)   10 (a bottle of juice),

c)   11 (2 glazed donuts),

d)   9 (2 plain donuts), or

e)   8 (1 fritter)

Which product provides the highest level of pleasure for this consumer? Coffee, at 15. So, the customer would spend his first buck on a cup of coffee.

But, of course, he has $2 yet to spend. What are his options for the second dollar?

He could buy coffee again, but of course, if he did, he would be consuming a second cup of coffee; so the marginal utility of a second cup of coffee, according to the chart, is 9.

And, then all of the previous options return for re-consideration. That is, he could consume some juice, and the marginal utility for consuming an initial bottle of juice is 10, or he could consume 2 glazed donuts which yield 11 (6 + 5), or he could purchase 2 plain donuts that would generate a level of pleasure of 9 (5 + 4), or he could consume his first fritter and get a pleasure level of 8.

So, for his second dollar, his options would be:

a)   9 (a second cup of coffee),

b)   10 (a bottle of juice),

c)   11 (2 glazed donuts),

d)   9 (2 plain donuts), or

e)   8 (1 fritter)

Of these alternatives, eating 2 glazed donuts brings the most enjoyment.

Hence, so far, he spends the first dollar on a cup of coffee, and he buys a couple of glazed donuts with the second dollar. What about dollar #3?

What are the options?

He could buy a second cup of coffee; that would yield a marginal utility of 9.

He could buy juice for the first time; that would yield a marginal utility of 10.

He could buy 2 more glazed donuts, i.e. glazed donuts 3 and 4, which would yield a combined marginal utility of 4 (2 + 2).

Or, he could consume his first fritter which would give a pleasure level of 8.

Which product yields the highest marginal utility? Yes, the juice at 10.

Therefore, the $3 would be spent on a cup of coffee, 2 glazed donuts, and 1 bottle of juice.

Given the recent narrative discussion, perhaps the matrix below will help summarize the options and choices that were made:

Marginal Utilities Per Option Note: * Chosen option, i.e. highest marginal utility					
Spending Decisions	Coffee	Juice	Glazed Donuts	Plain Donuts	Fritter
First $	15*	10	6 + 5 - 11	5 + 4 = 9	8
Second $	9	10	6 + 5 = 11*	5 + 4 = 9	8
Third $	9	10*	2 + 2 = 4	5 + 4 = 9	8

In real life, individuals don't create charts to make judgments about how to spend money or time amongst competing options. When you have $10 in your wallet and wish to buy some snacks for the upcoming family movie night, you look at the grocery shelves to see what the product options are and the various prices; and, then you mentally assign anticipated "likes and dislikes" (marginal utilities) by each family member for potato chips, corn chips, popcorn, pretzels, and so on. And, of course the issue is complicated a bit by different styles of cooking strategies of the manufacturers, say of chips. One family member really likes BBQ flavored chips, but would eat regular chips. And, another family member prefers a particular company's chips over all others. And, one family member has no particular druthers. So, you look at prices, and given your perceived marginal utilities of options by various family members, you make your choices. (How many times have you come home with bags of goodies only to receive a mixture of cheers and boos?)

The point to be made here is that economics is all about making choices, and we make choices "on the margin." Different people have different levels of enjoyment among product alternatives, and we have different amounts of pleasure as we consume more and more of the same item. So, the next time you go on a week long vacation with your family, and arrive at your destination, how will it be determined "who does what on which day"? Whether you realize it or not, the activities of each day of vacation will be determined by each family member's marginal utilities of the available options, and then some discussion (negotiation?) about those preferred options. Fun, fun, fun.

PRICE ELASTICITY

Now we need to shift gears. We need to cease thinking like a consumer, a "demander", and start thinking like a supplier. And, one of the more important questions a business supplier considers is what price should be assigned to a product or service when seeking to sell the item competitively. Such a query forces us to ponder the economic concept of *price elasticity*.

Price Elasticity: how responsive will consumers be when a price is changed.

—

In economics, elasticity means "responsiveness", that is, if a supplier changes its price on the product it sells, how will consumers react? If the price is lowered, will the company get more customers? Will existing customers buy more? Will any increase in demand by consumers be enough to more than offset the decreased revenue from a reduced price per sale? Conversely, if the organization raises its price, will it lose sales? But, even if it does, will the reduced demand be minor compared to the increased revenue from the increase in the selling price? All of that depends upon how responsive consumers are to increases/decreases in business prices. How elastic is the demand for that particular product?

Fortunately, we have a formula that can used to determine whether a price change depicts an elastic or an inelastic demand for that product; that formula is:

$$\frac{\dfrac{Q2 - Q1}{\dfrac{(Q2 + Q1)}{2}}}{\dfrac{P2 - P1}{\dfrac{(P2 + P1)}{2}}}$$

Where:

Q2   = the quantity demanded after the price has been changed (increased/decreased)

Q1   = the quantity demanded before the price was changed

P2   = the price after it was changed (increased/decreased)

P1   = the initial price before it was changed

Notice that the formula is nothing but one big fraction; indeed, it is one fraction on top of another fraction. The numerator is a fraction that is concerned with calculating a rate of change regarding consumer demand, a change in quantity purchased by consumers at two different prices, and the denominator is also a fraction concerned with calculating the rate of change in the price of the product in question. Therefore, the formula is simply calculating two rates of change and comparing them to one another. In the numerator, we are determining that responsiveness. How much did the consumers react to the price change? The denominator is calculating the rate of change in the price. Which rate is higher than the other? Or, more accurately, did the rate of responsiveness by consumers (the numerator) keep up with the rate of change in the price (the denominator)?

When all is said and done, there are only 3 possible outcomes when using the formula:

- If the numerator is greater than the denominator, the numerical answer to the formula will be some number that is greater than 1. When the answer is a number greater than 1, we call that situation "elastic."

- Should the numerator be equal to the denominator, which means the rate of change in consumer responsiveness was exactly equal to the rate of change in the decreased/increased price, (the answer to the formula is one), we call that scenario "unitary." (One American euphemism might be "a wash.")

- And, if the numerator turns out to be less than the denominator, that is, the rate of reaction by consumer demand is less than the rate of change in the price, the answer will be a number less than one and that situation is labeled as "inelastic."

So, to summarize the options, we could use the following chart:

Possible Answers	Product Demands	Reaction to Consumers to Price Change
> 1	Elastic	Consumers are responsive to the price change
= 1	Unitary	" a wash"
< 1	Inelastic	Not much change in consumer reaction when a price changes

Let's use 3 examples to illustrate.

First, assume you are selling cotton candy at a local county fair. At first, you try selling the product at $1.00, and you sell, on, average, 40 units an hour on the first day of the fair. You decide to see what happens if you lower the price to $.90, and you sell an average of 50 units a hour on the second day. Does the demand for your product seem to be elastic, unitary, or inelastic?

Using the price elasticity formula, we get:

$$\cfrac{\cfrac{50 - 40}{\dfrac{(50 + 40)}{2}}}{\cfrac{90 - 100}{\dfrac{(90 + 100)}{2}}} = \cfrac{\dfrac{10}{45}}{\dfrac{10}{95}} = \frac{.22}{.11} = 2 \quad (\text{elastic})$$

Notice that while the rate of change in the price was 11%, the rate of responsiveness by the consumers was 22%; hence, the reduced price was more than offset by the increase in sales to more customers.

How about another situation: Let's say that you sell chocolate covered ice cream bars at the local county fair. You initially sell at $5 a piece, and you sell, on average, 75 an hour on the first day. You opt to reduce your price to $3 an ice cream bar, and your sales improve to 125 units per hour, on average, the second day. Are you better off?

Using the formula, we get:

$$\dfrac{\dfrac{125 - 75}{(125 + 75)}}{\dfrac{2}{\dfrac{3 - 5}{(3 + 5)}}} = \dfrac{\dfrac{50}{100}}{\dfrac{2}{4}} = \dfrac{\dfrac{1}{2}}{\dfrac{1}{2}} = 1 \quad \text{(unitary)}$$

So, in this instance, the effort was "a wash." The reduced price caused more sales, but not enough additional sales to offset the reduced price.

Lastly, what if you sold foot long hotdogs at the fair? Your first price was $4 and you sold, on average, 10 an hour. You decided to cut the price on half and sell them at $2 instead the following day. Sales during the next day were, on average, 15 units per hour. Was the price change a smart move?

Again, using the elasticity formula, we get:

$$\dfrac{\dfrac{15 - 10}{(15 + 10)}}{\dfrac{2}{\dfrac{2 - 4}{(2 + 4)}}} = \dfrac{\dfrac{5}{12.5}}{\dfrac{2}{3}} = \dfrac{.40}{.67} = .06 \quad \text{(inelastic)}$$

Was it a profitable change? Nope. Consumers bought more hotdogs, but not nearly enough more to offset the reduction in price.

Can you now begin to see why a seller would like to know whether he is selling a product that tends to have an elastic or an inelastic demand? If the demand for the product is elastic, i.e. consumers are quite responsive to changes in price, then a reduction in price, if possible, is likely to be met with increased sales that are sufficient to offset the change in price. But, a raise in price is likely to be met with disgruntled customers who will seek to obtain other options.

If the supplier is selling a product with an inelastic demand, then lowering the price would actually be rather unwise. There is no need to be afraid of an increase in the price since the demand for the product is rather high (or constant) no matter what the actual price is. (Gasoline for automobiles is a good example; lowering the price won't cause consumers to drive lots more, and raising the price won't cause lot of Americans to drive lots less. There will be some reactions, but not in the rates that occur when prices are changed.)

CHAPTER SUMMARY

Recall from chapter 1 that economics is about making choices, and marginal utility is the essence of the decision-making process. People make choices among options based upon the perceived amounts of pleasures that the options will provide, including choices between first time experiences and products/services that are often consumed.

Price elasticity (of demand) concerns the responsiveness of consumers as suppliers raise or lower prices. If the rate of response by consumers is greater than the rate of the price change, the demand for that product is said to be elastic, and if the rate of response by consumers is less than the rate of the change in the price, the demand is said to be inelastic. (If the rates of change are the same, the demand is unitary, i.e. "a wash.") When seeking to determine if a price change is wise, suppliers care very much if the demand for their product seems to be elastic or inelastic; they need to anticipate the customer's reaction.

▶▶| *Chapter 6 Review*

Key concepts:

1. Utility regards the amount of joy or satisfaction that consumers gain from consuming products and services.

2. Marginal utility is the term used to describe the extra amount of joy or satisfaction that a consumer gains from consuming one more of a particular product or service.

3. Consumers make product or service selections based upon maximizing the amount of marginal utility gained from their product/service choices.

4. Price elasticity regards the responsiveness of consumers to changes in price.

5. Sellers are concerned about the consumer reactions to price changes and need to know whether the demand for their product/service is elastic, unitary, or inelastic.

6. An elastic demand means that the responsiveness of consumers is rather/quite high, i.e. the rate of change in customer consumption is higher than the rate of change in the price. Therefore, a seller's reduction in price can be expected to cause a significant increase in quantities purchased which should more than offset the revenue lost due to the price reduction. Conversely, sellers of elastic demand products should be leery of raising prices since consumers are likely to respond by purchasing significantly less.

7. A unitary demand means that the rate of change in a seller's price was merely matched by the rate of change in consumer purchases. There is no financial gain or loss to a seller by raising or lowering the price of a product with a unitary demand.

8. An inelastic demand means that the consumers are rather unresponsive to changes in the seller's price. So, the quantities purchased will not vary much if the seller increases/decreases its price.

Key terms:

utility, marginal utility, price elasticity

CHAPTER 07

MARKET STRUCTURES

While most of the topics in this economics fundamentals text are macroeconomic subjects, the subject of market structures is a microeconomic one, and a discussion that business and marketing professionals dissect in great detail. If you are an entrepreneur or a marketing manager, you may be disappointed that a working knowledge is all we will accomplish here. But, for most adult students, a firm foundation in this basic economic concept is highly desirable and potentially practical.

Market Structure: refers to combination of factors that create different selling conditions.

MARKET STRUCTURES

In economics, the term *market structure* refers to the combination of characteristics that comprise different competitive environments in which businesses operate, and there are 4 major competitive environments, i.e. market structures: 1) perfect competition, 2) monopolistic competition, 3) oligopoly, and 4) monopoly. And, these four market structures are separate competitive environments because each is composed of a different combination of characteristics. Let's use the matrix below as our basis for this chapter's discussion:

Notice that the left side column does not regard market structure options, but rather highlights the factors that cause different market environments to develop. While other economic sources will indicate a few other characteristics than those noted, the factors cited in the matrix are indeed the primary characteristics worth our consideration.

Market Structure Characteristics

Environmental Factors	Perfect Competition	Monopolistic Competition	Oligopoly	Monopoly
# of Sellers	too many	many	few	one
Uniqueness of Product	none	some	some	some/lots
Impact on Price	none	some	lots	"total"
Ease of Entry Into Market	easy	easy	hard	hard

Number of suppliers is perhaps the easiest factor for students to understand. While a monopoly means that there is only one (or one significantly dominant entity), perfect competition's key characteristic is that there are too many sellers, (an excess of competition). The oligopolistic market structure has but a few, though a few can mean, three or four, seven to ten (several). Monopolistic competition, the most common market structure of the four, has plenty of competition – not too much, but enough.

An additional factor is the uniqueness of the product the suppliers sell. For the perfect competition structure, there is nothing unique about the product; every seller's product pretty much looks like every other seller's product. Sizes may be a bit different, but the basic feature, color, shape, and so on are the same. But, sellers in the monopolistic competition market structure can make at least minor adjustments so as to create some uniqueness (product differentiation) of their products, and sellers in the oligopolistic market structure can similarly create sufficiently varied features in their respective product offerings. For the monopolistic market structure, the question is a moot one if there is literally only one company selling the item, but if there are a few competitive firms, with one either chosen (and regulated by the government) or dominant (but not yet deemed a true monopoly by the government), there is usually some product differentiation among the few business options in the monopoly environment.

The third, and key, factor that differentiates the four market structures is how much influence the sellers have over the price of the products they sell. Indeed, the previous two characteristics – the number of competitive sellers in the market, and the uniqueness of the sellers' products – combine to determine how much impact on its prices the sellers actually have. Hence, if there are too many sellers with nothing unique about the product, sellers have no control over the price. But, the many competitors in the monopolistic competition market structure can have some impact on their prices since they have some differentiation in their products. Sellers in an oligopolistic market structure have even more influence and control over prices since they, too, have some product differentiation, and there are relatively few of them. The seller in a monopolistic market structure has no immediate competition, so it can determine its own price, but such sellers are usually regulated by government, so their price must gain bureaucratic approval.

Lastly, the ease of entry into the competitive environment is a factor that helps form the market structure. If possible, businesses would hope to create barriers to prevent new competitors from starting, but such barriers are not feasible for the perfect competition and monopolistic competition market structures. However, one of the reasons there are few firms in the oligoplistic market structure is that it is not easy for a new firm to enter the oligopolist's world. Sometimes legal protections such as patents, trademarks, and copyrights provide an edge that newcomers cannot duplicate, and the start-up costs to compete in an oligopoly are usually too high for most entrepreneurs. Hence, the few oligopolistic competitors keep expenses high to keep future competitors out. And, a monopolist, if not selected and thereby given legal preference among competitors by a government body, has such a dominant market share that other (small by comparison) competitors don't pose much of a threat. Many emerging markets, often prompted by a new product invention, have a few competing firms, but one becomes controlling and captures the lion's share of consumers' interest.

But, we need to discuss these four market structures in greater detail.

MARKET STRUCTURES:

Perfect competition:

Perfect competition markets are markets with two important features. First, the demand for the product is huge and, second, the suppliers, though prolific, tend to be small. Agricultural products are perhaps the best examples. There are "thousands" of corn farms across the country, but one grower's bushel of corn is pretty much like another farmer's bushel of corn (within the same variety). If the product is strawberries, each of a thousand strawberry farmer's quart of strawberries looks essentially (size can vary some, but that's about it) like every other strawberry farmer's quart of product. But, just for a different example, anyone who has taken a Caribbean cruise knows that most island ports have downtown areas where a lot of wares are sold, including cheap t-shirts. Since every port has several t-shirt outlets, and there are several islands that cruising tourists can visit, the t-shirt market is a perfect competition market structure. So, regardless of which island city you visit, or which firm on the island of interest, you will be able to buy t-shirts at the same price (per category).

Perfect Competition: is a structure with no barriers and (too) many competitors.

But, whether oranges, apples, corn, wheat, cherries, catfish, or t-shirts, the important description is that the product demand is very substantial, and each supplier's product looks very much like any other supplier's product. Nothing unique. .

And, again, perfect competitive market structure firms are firms that face "hordes" of competition and sell a homogenous product, and because of those two overriding factors, such businesses are what economists call "price takers." That is, these firms cannot set their own prices; they are stuck with the prevailing price for their product that season. A perfect competition firm can't raise its price since it has plenty of competition and there's nothing special about its product to justify (in the mind of the consumer) a higher price. And, because the demand for the product far exceeds the firm's ability to supply it, the business can sell all it can produce at that prevailing price; hence, there is no benefit to lowering it. So, such firms must accept (take) the price level for the year (season). These firms can be quite profitable by controlling their costs, but they can't change their price(s).

Lastly, because the size and scope of these firms is usually small to moderate, there are no barriers to entering the market. Firms come and go with relative ease.

Monopolistic competition:

Monopolistic Competition: is a structure with no barriers, lots of competition, and some product uniqueness. While it is quite possible to make a profit in a perfect competition market structure, few firms wish to be in a perfect competition structure on purpose. Hence, most firms prefer to sell products that can be differentiated at least a little bit, so most of America's free enterprise occurs in the monopolistic competition market structure. There are plenty of competitors, even too many at times, but sellers are able to modify the features of their products so as to be able to sell their products at higher (or lower) prices.

Think about many of the products you purchase, and chances are high that the item can be produced with "generic" features or "luxurious, custom designed" features. And, chances are high that you can think of the seller that specializes in the low price option, and there are stores that promote the high(er) quality end of the spectrum. The product could be lawn mowers, sweaters, greeting cards, appliances, or watches, and you are accustomed to a product assortment based upon different features, abilities, benefits, and – price. The monopolistic competition market structure is where most of our economy resides.

Oligopoly:

Like monopolistic competition, firms in an oligopoly can differentiate their products from their competitors, but of course there are far fewer firms in an oligopoly. While monopolistic competitive market structures is where the majority of America does its business, the oligopolistic market structure is where businesses wish they could operate. Why can't most businesses operate in an oligopolistic market? Because of the barriers to entry. Those firms that are already in an oligopoly make it so expensive to be in it that the high cost of entry keeps most new competitors out. Indeed, the usual way a firm ever gets into an oligopoly is that the oligopoly was a monopolistic competition market structure in its earlier days, but as the demand for the product "caught on", a few were able to significantly increase production abilities and their operations grew along with the ever increasing demand. Some of the earlier competitors dropped out or remained small; only a few were able to significantly increase the scope of their operations.

Oligopoly: is a market structure with few competitors and some entry barriers.

Some of the most well known companies in American free enterprise operate in oligopolistic markets. For example, when it comes to the soda industry, how many firms are there? Ten to fifteen or so. But, how many are there really? Just two (Coca Cola and Pepsico). Or, when you think about breakfast cereal, how many competitors are there really? Kellogg's, General Mills, Post, Quaker Oats, and that's about it. And, oligopolies occur in markets ranging from greeting cards to automobile tires to canned soup. You and I buy goods from oligopolistic companies most every day; here's just a sample list:

Product or Service	Major Companies
Athletic Shoes	Nike, Adidas, Reebok
Baby Food	Gerber, Heinz, Beech-Nut
Batteries	Duracell, Eveready, Ray-O-Vac
Beer	Anheuser-Busch, Miller, Coors
Camera Film	Eastman Kodak, Polaroid, Fuji
Chewing Gum	Wrigley, Hershey, Pfitzer
Chocolate Candy	Hershey, Nestle, Mars, Brach
Credit Cards	Visa, Mastercard, Discover, Am. Express
Detergent	Proctor & Gamble, Colgate-Palmolive, Dial, Lever Bros
Greeting Cards	Hallmark, American Greetings, Gibson
Tires	Goodyear, Bridgestone/Firestone, B.F. Goodrich

Monopoly:

Near the end of the 19th Century, the country finally got fed up with several American corporations dominating the free enterprise system and Congress passed the Sherman Anti-Trust Act. Throughout much of the decades following the Civil War, leading firms in some of the countries major industries "banned" together to prevent or limit competition in their respective industries via interlocking

Monopoly: a market structure with 1 seller, usually regulated by government.

directorates, and the establishment of collusive trusts. In 1890, the U.S. Congress finally made monopolies (and such practices) illegal; the legislation specifically sought to target practices that reduced competition. The Sherman Anti-Trust Act only had two significant sections: 1) any contract or conspiracy to restrain trade was deemed illegal, and 2) monopolies or attempts to monopolize are illegal. The problem, of course, is that what constitutes "restraint of trade" or "a monopoly" is not a completely objective judgment, and part of our judicial history regards determining what actions truly and meaningfully damage competition.

Sadly, entrepreneurial shenanigans simply got more creative, and Congress needed to try again to prevent actions that unacceptably restricted competition, and the Clayton Act was passed in 1914. The major provisions prohibited: 1) price discrimination (sellers could not charge different buyers different prices for the same product), 2) tying contracts (sellers would require purchasers to buy one good (they didn't want) in order to buy another good (the one they did want), 3) exclusive dealing (sellers would require that its buyers could not also buy from their competitors), 4) mergers (one company could not acquire a competitor if the consequence would substantially decrease competition, and 5) interlocking directorates (the same person could not sit on the boards of competing companies).

The Federal Trade Commission was also created in 1914, and its role was to police various unacceptable business practices, but subsequent court rulings (saying that only the judiciary could decide what was unacceptable, unfair, inappropriate, etc.) reduced the FTC's focus on monitoring and preventing false and deceptive advertising.

Currently, an authorized monopoly is regulated by the government, most notably a public utility.

Lastly, many misunderstand the true power of a monopoly. People mistakenly believe that the "evil" associated with monopolies is that they can charge exorbitant prices. Not particularly true. Admittedly, since there is no competition, a monopoly firm can restrict supply and thereby sell at a price level higher than it might if it faced some direct competition. But, all products have at least some indirect competition. For example, a locally authorized cable television company wouldn't charge $100/month for a basic package even if the public service commission would approve it because at such a price, consumers would likely prefer to read a book, play in a local park, take a walk, visit local museums or theatres, and so on. While the cable television company has no other cable television competitors, it does have competition from other forms of entertainment.

Hence, the bigger disadvantage of a monopolistic firm (though not yet adjudicated as a monopoly) is that it can get away with selling at a higher price by limiting supply. There is little benefit to the monopolist for increasing supply as it will only serve to lower its selling price, but the lower price won't generate sufficient additional sales to make it worth doing. Hence, the monopolist is in the enviable position of determining on its own what output levels and subsequent prices will yield the highest profits. The monopolistic firm will need to know how elastic/inelastic its product is, but the monopolistic firm will be able to sell lower quantities for higher prices than would be the case if direct competition existed.

CHAPTER SUMMARY

American free enterprise is built on competition; we believe that competition keeps prices lower than they would otherwise be, and competition leads to innovation and even invention. But not all product/ service industries have the same volume of competition; some have essentially too much, while others may not have enough. Sometimes the very nature of the product or service creates the amount of competition in that industry, but entrepreneurial greediness can also seek to limit competition in particular industries. We can characterize those levels of competition with the concept called market structure which indicates the likely level of competition according to four factors: 1) the number of competitors in that industry, 2) the uniqueness of the product/service sold in that industry, 3) the ability of competitors to influence their product/service price, and 4) the ease with which new competitors can enter the industry.

While most every business venture would no doubt prefer to operate in an oligopolistic market, the bulk of American free enterprise occurs in monopolistic competitive markets.

▶▶ *Chapter 7 Review*

Key concepts:

1. A market structure refers to the features of an industry that ultimately determine the level of competition in that industry.

2. The basic features that describe an industry are: 1) number of firms in the industry, 2) uniqueness of the product or service in that industry, 3) the impact that competitors in that industry can have on their product's price, and 4) what barriers, if any, there may be to entering/exiting that industry.

3. A Perfect Competition market structure is characterized by:

    a. Too many competitors
    b. Very large demand for the product; suppliers are small as well as too many

    c.   No uniqueness of the product or service

    d.   No influence on the product's price (for that season); firms are "price takers"

    e.   Relatively easy to enter the industry

Agriculture is a prime example of Perfect Competition market structures.

4.   A Monopolistic Competition market structure is characterized by:

    a.   Many competitors

    b.   Ability to alter product features so that there is some uniqueness of product

    c.   Some ability to impact price and charge for sellers' "unique" feature(s)

    d.   Relatively easy to enter the industry

Retail is a prime example of Monopolistic Competition market structures.

5.   An Oligopolistic market structure is characterized by:

    a.   Few(er) competitors

    b.   Ability to alter product features so that there is uniqueness of product

    c.   Higher ability to impact price because there is less competition as well as some product uniqueness

    d.   Difficult (very expensive) to enter the industry

Manufacturing is a prime example of Oligopolistic Competition market structures.

6.   A Monopolistic market structure is characterized by:

    a.   One (regulated) competitor

    b.   Ability to alter product features to create some uniqueness of product

    c.   Price approved by a government entity, e.g. Public Service Commission

Public utilities (e.g. power/light, cable TV) are prime examples.

Key terms:

Market structure, perfect competition, monopolistic competition, oligopoly, monopoly

CHAPTER 08

PRODUCTION AND MARGINAL REVENUE & MARGINAL COST

As we saw in the previous chapter, different market structures impact a business's ability to influence or control its selling price. Because there are so many competitors in an industry whose product looks the same, a perfect competition business has no way to self-determine its selling price and is, indeed, a price taker. Because businesses in monopolistic competition and oligopoly market structures can alter the features of their product offerings, they can have modest to significant influence on their selling prices. And, lastly, a monopoly has complete control over its selling price – but it must gain governmental approval of the price before pursuing sales with it. Hence, a business' control over its sales depends a great deal on its industry and market structure dynamics.

But, what a business *can* control is its costs. Business operations require inventory or raw materials, equipment, labor, land, and policies and procedures that combine to yield a produced good ready to sell to a customer, and businesses (should) pay close attention to the organization's efficiency and productivity. Typically, the more efficient the business operations, the lower the unit cost of the firm's good or service (which may enable the firm to sell at a lower price), and the higher the productivity, the higher the organization's profits. So, a firm's ultimate profitability often has a lot to do with its ability to manage its costs.

CATEGORIES of EXPENSES

Variable Expense:
is a cost that varies as sales vary.

All costs (expenses) can be placed in one of two broad categories: variable and fixed. Let's clarify.

Variable Expenses

Variable expenses are those costs that vary, that is, they change as the firm's sales volume changes. For example, the only way for a retail shoe store to sell more shoes is for it to first buy more shoes from its wholesaler or manufacturers. Or, conversely, if the retailer assumes that he will sell fewer shoes over the upcoming "slow period," he will merely cut back on his orders for shoes from his wholesaler or manufacturers. Hence, inventory purchases can increase in anticipation of expected increases in retail shoe sales, and inventory purchase can be curtailed as retail sales slow. The expense called inventory varies (increases or decreases) as the sales activity changes.

Similarly, if you owned a small pizza store, all of your raw materials for making pizzas would be variable costs. The more pizzas you need to sell, the more pepperoni, sausage, tomato paste, cheese, and so on you will need to obtain first. If pizza sales are likely to be down for a period, you minimize your expenses by buying fewer raw materials in the first place. Again, costs associated with making the product can adjust to the expected sales volume.

Other types of variable expenses include office supplies and deliveries.

Fixed Expenses

Fixed costs, on the other hand, are expenses that do not change as the sales volume changes. While all costs eventually change, since no expenses are always "fixed," we nevertheless use the label to describe those expenses that remain constant (at least in the short run) even though the sales activity is rising or falling.

Except for large businesses that own the land on which they operate, most firms pay rent to some landowner. Think of your favorite shopping mall. There may be a big "anchor" store at one end (often a mall has 2-3 anchor stores), but most of the various stores are small businesses with very few employees. These stores have rental agreements with the mall owner, usually a company that built the mall. And, these rental agreements typically stipulate that the store pay a monthly sum to the mall owner for the duration of the lease. The rent is some constant amount each month; the store owner needs to pay that monthly sum whether it has a million customers or no customers.

That is, rent is a cost that does not vary even though the sales activity may change.

Such fixed expenses are often labeled as *overhead,* and a variety of common business expenses fall into this category such as insurance, depreciation, mortgages and loans, and property taxes.

Fixed Expense: is a cost that does not vary as sales vary.

One key expense that can be difficult to categorize is labor. Personnel expenses are usually treated as fixed in the short run as firms seek to gain productivity increases with the same number of employees, but if sales increases continue, additional workers will be added eventually. So, in the short run, labor is often treated as a fixed expense, but then becomes a variable expense in the long run.

Explicit Versus Implicit Costs

One other distinction between expenses needs to be highlighted. When most people think of the production process, they think of workers interacting with machines that create some sort of assembly line procedure. And, it's certainly true that production costs include the expenses of labor, materials, equipment, capital, and so on, but it is also true that there are other kinds of expenses that should be considered by the entrepreneur or business owner when assessing the production function in his/her firm.

The word *explicit* means "clear" or "unequivocal", i.e. something is articulated in detail. So, explicit costs are costs that are outlined in some sort of contract or agreement. Labor expenses are sometimes contained in contractual language while other labor "agreements" are merely at-will employment handshakes. Costs for machines and equipment are typically evidenced by some sort of purchase order made to acquire the asset(s). The value of raw materials or borrowed money (capital) is stipulated in paperwork agreements. So, these normal examples of expenses are explicit costs, that is, they are valued according to some agreement or contract.

Explicit Cost: is a cost that results from a contract or an agreement.

Recall the concept of opportunity cost. When business entrepreneurs opt to use their savings to start a venture, those savings could have been used for a different purpose, or even just placed into a savings account. Or, the entrepreneur has now devoted their time to operating this business, but the individual could have used his/her time in other potentially valuable ways. And, because entrepreneurs assume risk with their time and money, a certain amount of minimum profit is required in their minds for the endeavor to be "worth it." These forgone opportunities and minimum requirements represent some examples of *implicit* costs, that is, expenditures for which there is no exact corresponding cash payment.

Implicit Cost: is a cost of a foregone opportunity.

From an accounting point of view, only explicit costs are considered when measuring costs of production, profits and losses, and so on. But, from the business owner's point of view, forgone opportunities and personal financial expectations "count" when determining success.

MARGINAL REVENUE and MARGINAL COST

Marginal Revenue: additional revenue from selling 1 more.

Marginal Cost: additional cost from producing 1 more.

Profit for an organization is of course Revenue minus Expenses. Revenue comes from sales of a firm's products, interest income from any investments, and so on, and expenses involve any cash outflows for raw materials, equipment and supplies, utilities, workers, loan payments, depreciation, taxes, and so on. Add up all the sales (revenue) and any investment income, add up all the expenses, and subtract the expense total from the revenue total; *voila!* Profit (we hope).

But, from the production manager's (and the business manager's) perspective, what should be even more important is an analysis of the company's *marginal revenue* and *marginal cost* for producing the firm's products. You may recall from a previous chapter (on Marginal Utility) that the word marginal means extra or incremental amount. So, marginal revenue concerns how much additional revenue is received by the company when it sells one more item. And, then another. And, then another. Again, you may recall from a previous chapter (on Market Structures) that firms do not always sell all of their products for the same price even when it is the same product. At any rate, *marginal revenue* refers to the extra amount of revenue the company receives when it sells one more product item. For example, if my total revenue is $115 for selling 9 units, and my revenue becomes $125 when selling 10 units, the marginal revenue for the 10th unit is $10.

Similarly, *marginal cost* refers to the additional cost the company experiences when it sells one more product item. Marginal costs reflect both variable costs and fixed costs (and fixed costs include expenses in machinery and equipment), so marginal costs tend to be high(er) at low volumes of output (because the equipment expense is "spread" over relatively few items, but marginal costs decrease as output increases since the fixed equipment costs can be spread over larger production amounts. But, just to cite one example, if the firm's total cost for producing nine units was $100, and then the total cost became $107 when producing 10 items, the marginal cost of producing the 10th unit is $7.

While the firm is certainly interested in its total profit from all of the company's departments and operations, it will want to pay special attention to the firm's output levels because output levels will be a major determinant of the organization's overall profitability. And, major factors in determining the appropriate output level are the firm's marginal revenue and marginal cost figures. We turn to that discussion next.

The Production Function and Maximum Profitability

When discussing revenue, costs, and profits, I ask my students to tell me how much should a firm produce to be profitable. And, invariably, students will say, "well, the firm should produce as much as it can, of course!" And, that would be wrong. J The answer to the question, "at what output level should a business produce so as to maximize its profits" is found in the answer, "where MR = MC." (In reality, it is rare that MR actually equals MC, so one is looking for the output level where MR and MC come closest to being equal, yet MR is higher.) Hence, the output level where the company's marginal revenue is most closely matched by its marginal cost is the output level that will generate the highest profits. And, we should now ask for the assistance of what is called a Production Function to illustrate the point.

A Production Function is really just a chart, or a table of needed information. See the example table below (Figure 8-1).

Production Function for Tom's Toy Trains

Output	TC	ATC	MC	TR	ATR	MR Loss	Profit/
0	$100.00	-	-	-	-	-	<$100.00>
1	116.66	116.66	16.66	30.00	30.00	30.00	<86.66>
2	130.76	65.38	14.10	60.00	30.00	30.00	<70.76>
3	140.60	46.87	9.84	90.00	30.00	30.00	<50.60>
4	145.24	36.31	4.64	120.00	30.00	30.00	<25.24>
5	150.00	30.00	4.76	150.00	30.00	30.00	< 0.00>
6	157.16	26.19	7.16	180.00	30.00	30.00	22.84
7	166.82	23.83	9.66	210.00	30.00	30.00	43.18
8	181.16	22.70	14.78	240.00	30.00	30.00	58.84
9	201.18	22.35	20.02	270.00	30.00	30.00	68.82
10	229.85	22.99	28.67	300.00	30.00	30.00	70.15
11	265.18	24.11	35.33	330.00	30.00	30.00	64.82
12	312.67	26.06	47.49	360.00	30.00	30.00	47.33
13	371.54	28.58	58.87	390.00	30.00	30.00	18.46
14	443.82	31.70	72.28	420.00	30.00	30.00	<23.82>
15	533.05	35.64	89.23	450.00	30.00	30.00	<83.05>

Let's review the table.

First, the column on the left merely indicates the various levels of potential output. In reality, the output level is much more than 15, but it is shortened to help make the bigger points we need to present.

Second, TC stands for Total Cost, that is, the respective fixed expenses and variable expenses have been combined together into a total sum. (But, from our example data, it is evident that the fixed expense for this toy train is $100 since the company incurs this expense even when no trains are produced. When the company begins to produce trains, the fixed expenses are added to the variable expenses to arrive at the total cost at each level of production output.)

Next, though we don't need to concern ourselves with it in our application, most production and business managers want to keep track of the average cost to produce an item at various output levels, so ATC regards that statistic.

Fourth, MC stands for Marginal Cost, one of the two concepts we are definitely interested in for our illustration. Again, marginal means extra or additional amount, so the MC sum is merely the change in TC when producing one more toy train. For instance, the total cost (TC) for making 3 trains is $140.60, and the total cost (TC) for making 4 toy trains is $145.24; hence, the marginal cost (MC) for making one more train (train #4) is $145.24 minus $140.60, or the $4.64 cited in the MC column. Notice that, while the numbers continue to consistently rise in the TC column, the figures in the MC column initially decline before then increasing to sums that exceed the price the firm is selling its toy train for.

We then shift to the revenue columns. TR stands for total revenue, ATR regards the average revenue at various output levels, and MR is the second column of our special interest, i.e. marginal revenue. Clearly, Tom's Toy Trains sells its product for the same price, $30, no matter how many are produced and sold. Therefore, the TR column is nothing more than $30 times the output level, and the average and marginal revenue figures are just a reflection of the ever same selling price of $30. Thus, every time another train is sold, the extra or additional revenue is always $30.

So, at what output level is Tom's Toy Trains the most profitable? According to our formula, the answer should be where MR = MC (or where we can get as close to it with MR still a bit higher than MC). We know that the MR figure of $30 never changes, so all we really need to do is look down the MC column to see if there is a figure of $30. You will note that $30 does not appear in the MC column, so this is one of those examples where we need to come as close as we can. You will find a MC sum of $28.67 (the closest we get to $30 without "going over"), and indeed, if you subsequently look at the far right column for Profit/ Loss figures, you will also see that $70.15 is the highest profit sum.

Thus, if the question is "at what output level will Tom's Toy Trains maximize its profits", the answer is 10. The firm will be profitable at other output levels, e.g., at output nine or output 11, but neither level will be as high as the profit at level 10. A firm's profit is maximized when its **marginal** cost is equal to (or slightly below) its **marginal** revenue at that output level.

(By the way, what is the firm's break even output level?)

Break Even Point:

Business owners and managers utilize a handy planning tool called the "Break Even Point" calculation. Firms incur a variety of expenses, and they of course hope to make a profit each month, but a common strategy for organizations is to establish sales goals (sales quotas) which, if hit, rather ensures that the business will be profitable for that period of time, i.e. month, quarter, or year. But, how do such targets get established in the first place? The usual answer is the Break Even Point.

The purpose of the Break Even Point is to calculate the number of units that the firm will need to sell to just cover its costs, i.e. break even. No profit. But, also no loss. And, the formula for calculating the Break Even Point is:

$$\text{B.E. point} = \frac{\text{Fixed Costs}}{\text{Selling price} - \left(\dfrac{\text{Variable costs}}{\text{Units sold}}\right)}$$

So, again, let's use an example to demonstrate its helpfulness. Paul is an excellent cook, and he believes that he has the ability to make delicious pizzas. So, Paul starts Paul's Pizza Palace (as a pizza take-out restaurant); he estimates his sales and expenses for the 6 months to be:

	January	February	March	April	May	June
PAUL'S PIZZA PALACE **Income Statement Data**						
Sales (Avg. price is $10/pizza)	$ 6,000	$ 8,000	$10,000	$10,000	$12,000	$15,000
Ingredients	1,500	2,000	2,500	2,500	3,000	4,000
Heat	300	400	500	500	600	750
Mileage	200	300	400	400	500	650
Store rent	1,000	1,000	1,000	1,000	1,000	1,000
Lights	50	50	50	50	50	50
Phone	100	100	100	100	100	100
Lease: 2 ovens	200	200	200	200	200	200
Lease: 1 refrig	100	100	100	100	100	100
Labor – 2	2,500	2,500	2,500			
Labor – 3				3,500	3,500	3,500

As I suggested at the outset, the Break Even Point is a planning tool that helps managers play what I call the "what if" game. Once monthly estimates of revenue and expenses are made, such as above, the break even point for each month can be determined; and, once determined, there are really only 3 possible outcomes: 1) no problem "piece of cake," the firm can easily meet the needed sales volume, 2) maybe; "it will probably be close, and we will need to keep a close eye on everything, but if we use a little of this and a little of that, we might be able to reach that goal", or 3) not possible; "no way." Except that, "the third option (and even the second option) assumed an estimate of expenses, but what if the firm made some changes (probably to reduce some costs)? Could the business reach the new break-even point? Therefore, a business manager will calculate the break- even point, given current expense estimates, and then decide whether any changes might be needed to be in a better position to reach a break-even volume. ("What if we did this? What if we did that?")

Using Paul's estimates, what is the break-even point for January? How many pizzas will Paul need to sell to break even in January? Recall our discussion earlier in this chapter regarding the difference between variable and fixed expenses and realize that Paul's "income statement" has nicely segmented the variable costs (pizza ingredients, heat for cooking the pizzas, etc.) from the fixed costs (rent, lights, etc.) Notice also that labor is "fixed" for the initial 3 months, and then Paul opts to hire another employee so that the labor expense increases to a new "fixed" sum for the last three months.

For January, the break even point (# of pizzas needing to be sold) is:

$$BE = \frac{3,950}{10 - \left(\frac{2,000}{600*}\right)} = \frac{3,950}{10 - 3.33} = \frac{3,950}{6.67} = 592$$

(* sales/selling price)

So, would the firm be profitable? Yes, but not by much. Given those figures, the pizza palace expects to sell 600 pizzas, just 8 pizzas over its break even point. (That's why the firm only had $50 in profit.)

How about the expectations for February? Does Paul need to think about making any serious changes? Let's see.

$$BE = \frac{3,950}{10 - \left(\frac{2,700}{800}\right)} = \frac{3,950}{10 - 3.38} = \frac{3,950}{6.62} = 596$$

The financial picture improved; while the break-even point rose to 596 (because the variable costs were higher than the month before), they also expected to sell more pizzas, –800-- (up from 600 the month before). Hence, the projection is that the firm will be able to sell over 200 more pizzas than required.

Let me encourage you to actually calculate the remaining monthly break-even points (repetition is a good teacher), but Paul could summarize his estimates thusly:

	January	February	March	April	May	June
BE point.	592	596	598	750	752	773
Estimated Sales volume	600	800	1,000	1,000	1,200	1,500
Unit cost	$3.33	$3.38	$3.40	$3.40	$3.42	$3.60
Profit	$50	$1,350	$2,650	$1,650	$2,950	$4,650

(Just for fun, while the business is clearly becoming more and more profitable over the 6 months (assuming Paul's estimates are reasonably accurate), can you spot a potential problem? (Hint: though Paul seems to have no difficulty in selling enough pizzas each month, how much is it costing him to make one? Business managers note such things.)

At any rate, the Break Even Point can help a business leader decide whether operational adjustments may be necessary. Given estimates of current expenses and the calculation of the needed break even volume to cover those expenses, decision-makers can better determine whether any changes will be needed to reach needed sales targets.

CHAPTER SUMMARY:

For this chapter, we put on our business manager hat and looked at a couple of foundational concepts entrepreneurs use to plan operations which will cause expenses to be experienced, but also, profits to be maximized.

The Production Function enables a business manager to determine what production level (and the expenses incurred at that level) will produce the highest possible profit, and maximizing profits does not usually mean producing at maximum output.

And, the Break Even Point calculation enables a business manager to decide if any operational changes are in order to facilitate a sales volume that the firm can better (or more easily) achieve.

▶▶| Chapter 8 Review

Key concepts:

1. Expenses are categorized into two groups: 1) variable and 2) fixed.

2. Costs (expenses) can also be perceived as explicit or implicit costs.

3. A Production Function can be used to determine a firm's output level that maximizes its profit.

4. The Break Even Point calculation enables a manager decide if changes in operations will be needed to at least cover expenses.

Key terms:

variable expense, fixed expense, explicit cost, implicit cost, marginal revenue, marginal cost

CHAPTER 09

MONEY BASICS

Years ago I gave my economics students the following "surprise quiz" question:

> There once was an upright and very proper Englishman, who regularly took his summer vacation on a tiny, agreeable Aegean island. The Englishman had returned to the island so many times that his trust-worthiness had been established beyond any possible doubt. There was absolutely no chance that this Englishman's bank would fail to honor his checks, and, indeed, all of them had always been honored promptly.
>
> Since the Englishman's credit was so sound, the islanders were totally happy to allow him to pay by check, with the certain knowledge that they were good checks. Indeed, so well-known and trusted was the Englishman on this tiny island that the islanders were happy to accept the Englishman's checks from one another. For example, if the restaurant wished to pay the grocer partly with a check he had received in payment for a meal, the grocer was happy to accept the check. The grocer was able to buy gas with the check, and the Englishman's checks circulated in this way around the island. In-deed the checks were never returned to the Englishman's London bank for collection.
>
> Who paid for the Englishman's holiday?

The answer to the question, of course, is that island vendors paid for the Englishman's vacation since his "payment" was never redeemed. His purchases were free, though he did not realize it at the time. But, more importantly, the concept worth noting here is that money can take on many forms, and in this instance, the Englishman's check became like currency to the islanders.

WHAT IS MONEY?

Money:
anything that
enables a
transaction.

Money is defined as *a medium of exchange*, that is, money is anything that can help facilitate a transaction. As the example above indicates, money can be anything that is widely accepted; as long as most everyone is comfortable with accepting it as payment for products sold or services rendered, the actual form of the money can be whatever people want it to be. Pieces of metal (coins made of gold, silver, and more recently, copper and nickel), pieces of paper (currency, checks), pieces of plastic (credit cards and debit cards), chunks of salt, strings of beads, skins of selected animals (beaver pelts and buffalo hides), and even rolls of tobacco have all been used as money.

"We All Want Money Because We All Want Money"

Actually, the above sentiment is not gobbledygook; it is a truism. The choice of a monetary form is discretionary, but the key is to choose a form of money in which the users have confidence. People don't actually want the money; they want the items that the money can buy. We don't want pieces of paper (currency) or pieces of metal (coins); we want the food, shoes, and so on that the money will purchase. But, why can you purchase groceries at the store with some cash, i.e. why is the grocer willing to take your cash? The answer is because he can, in turn, use your money to give to another party for something he wants; e.g. , compensate employees, pay the supplier for the boxes of cereal he ordered, and so on. The supplier, for example, accepts the money from the grocer because the supplier can use the money to pay his employees, pay the light bill with the local public utility company, pay the gas station for gas in his delivery trucks, and so on. Hence, the money simply facilitates the variety of transactions that people wish to make, and the only consideration that the parties truly care about is whether there is sufficient agreement in the acceptance of the actual form of money. Therefore, each of us wants money (whatever the specific form of it is) **because everyone else wants it, too.** We all want money because we all want money. We want whatever form everyone else wants.

How Is Confidence Developed?

Fiat Money:
is a medium
given value
by govern-
ment edict.

So, the real question is how does one generate public confidence in a form of money in the first place? When a country first starts, the basis of a money's acceptance is a government decree. *Fiat money* is money that is "given" value because the government says so. (Of course, if the government ceases to exist, the form of money may or may not continue to hold value.) In the United States, the government

Legal Tender:
is coins or
currency.

established currency and coins as our legal tender by passing legislation that obligated sellers and creditors to accept the legal tender, the fiat money, as payment for any purchase or debt. That essentially got the confidence ball rolling; the law basically said, "Accept these forms of money as payment for purchases or else the purchaser gets the goods for free." Over time, people just got accustomed to giving one another the forms of money in exchange for the goods or services they really wanted. Today, no one gives much thought to accepting it or not.

HISTORICAL FORMS of MONEY

Money is merely a "medium of exchange", that is, the purpose of money is to facilitate transactions. When actual, acceptable forms of money have not quite been established (think back to some old movies about frontier America), individuals used a *barter* system. Barter means that transactions occurred on the basis of negotiated trades between finished goods or services. A rugged fur trapper would walk into the general store in the frontier town and throw a pile of beaver pelts on the counter, and then seek to exchange some or all of them for some sacks of flour, cans of food, a jug of rum, a new pair of boots, and so on. If the store keeper was willing to accept furs as payment for goods, the two would begin to negotiate a deal. Sometimes an agreement was reached, and sometimes not.

Barter: is trading goods or services without the use of money.

Further, consider the farmer who grew livestock as well as crops. Just think of the planning that must be accomplished for the farmer to "sell" his cow for all of the items he wants in town. He must negotiate a deal with the blacksmith for part of the cow if he needs some horse repairs, another deal with the store clerk for part of his cow for food and clothing, yet another deal with the innkeeper if he was staying the night before returning home, and perhaps even another deal if he wanted a tab with the local bartender. And, only after all these acceptable arrangements for certain parts of the cow were made in advance would he then slaughter the cow. The more needs the farmer had, the more parties he would need to strike deals with; i.e., the more complicated the transaction of business became.

While clumsy, does barter still happen today? Sure. The most common examples usually occur between neighbors or friends. I might say to my friend, "I need to do some birthday (or holiday) shopping, so would you be willing to watch my kids for a couple of hours this weekend? In exchange, I will watch your kids for a couple of hours the following weekend." Or, I might say to my neighbor, "my lawnmower is on the fritz, and I see that you are about to mow your lawn. Would you be willing to mow my lawn if I wash your car next week?" Or, in my youth, I collected baseball cards, and I often engaged in trades of cards with my friends who also collected. Of course, you may have already spotted the challenge associated with bartering:—what constitutes a fair trade? While two neighbors may watch each other's children for the same length of time, what if one set of children are well-behaved and easy to monitor while the other family's children are brats and difficult to supervise? And, unless the lawn is quite small, I wouldn't suspect that one lawn mowing equals one car wash. (A lawn mowing may be more equal to 3 car washings.) And, a Mickey Mantle baseball card was always worth 2-3 cards of lesser known players – unless my friend had a card of a player on my favorite team. At any rate, while it can work, bartering requires negotiating respective values that may differ between the negotiating parties. It may be time- consuming or emotionally risky.

Creating money makes transactions easier to accomplish. After you acquire an asset of value, i.e. an animal skins, livestock, agricultural crops, hauls of fish, and so on, converting those assets into a form of money makes it easier for the trapper, farmer, fisherman, etc. to then buy the desired items at the local market. Once armed with whatever the acceptable forms of money are in that jurisdiction, the buyers can more easily decide if a purchase is feasible.

The earliest form of money was probably metal coins. Mostly because metals were relatively rare, and partly because the "precious" metals "sparkled" or were "shiny", gold and silver became the metal that individuals found acceptable. History indicates that the Egyptians first "minted" gold and silver coins, and the varying denominations of the coin depended upon how much gold and silver was put into the coin. Roman and Greek empires continued the practice. But, history also records that populations in various countries used beads, shells, gems (pearls, diamonds, rubies, and sapphires), tobacco, and even blocks of salt.

However, except for coins, commodity money, such as hides, shells, gems, and crops, would still have the same problems as barter. Not all beads were of the same size, and not all gems were of the same quality. And, if you happened to leave your salt outside, and it rained, your value could literally melt away.

The Middle Ages sowed the seeds for paper money, i.e. checks (bank notes). Consider the following example. Samuel, a brick layer, is asked by the local duke to fix some damage done to the castle wall by some nomadic marauders. After a couple of weeks, Samuel has completed the repairs and seeks his payment. But, in the meantime, the duke has injured his leg and is bed-ridden. But, the duke knows that he has some of his wealth stored in a safe with the village's blacksmith. (Blacksmiths needed safes to protect the metals that they would use in their work, and, while not common knowledge, the duke kept some of his treasure in the blacksmith's safe to access when he went to the village to shop.) So, the duke had an idea; he wrote a note which he gave to Samuel. The note said, "I hereby authorize the blacksmith shop to pay one hundred sovereigns from my account to the bearer of this note (Samuel)", and the duke's signature (and seal?) were his authorization. What did the duke just do? He wrote a check. A check is nothing more than an "authorization slip" (of blank lines to be filled in) to allow your banker to take some of your funds and give it to the holder of the note-. Perhaps the blacksmith already knew Samuel, or perhaps Samuel had a way of confirming his identity to a stranger, or perhaps the blacksmith wasn't concerned as long as he recognized the duke's signature, but the note simply authorized the blacksmith to give a specific sum of the duke's holdings to Samuel. That's how checks (bank notes) work. Checks reduce the need for carrying cash (thereby minimizing theft), and checks enable one to transact some business in various locations.

But, after checks were devised, it wasn't much of a stretch to then devise currency, paper money in separate denominations. The key is to print a volume of currency that would equal something of agreed upon intrinsic value. (Again, money can be whatever a society wants it to be as long as most everyone agrees to it. Widespread acceptance is required.) For centuries that "backing" was gold and silver, but modern economies no longer rely on them to underwrite their currencies. Gold and silver are still held in banks that serve international customers because the gold and silver serve as a source of confidence and comfort between companies in separate countries. Today, currencies in modern economies are backed by the countries' abilities to produce goods and services that others want.

Technology has created additional forms of money. Credit cards debuted in the 1960's, but only business executives and wealthy individuals had them. Rather than carry cash, such cardholders could use their Diner's Club or American Express card to pay for their expensive meals and vacations. Since credit cards are not legal tender, the cards could only be used at establishments that accepted them as payment; i.e., had a level of confidence in them. Eventually, of course, sellers became more and more willing to accept credit cards as payment for their goods and services, and the vast majority of Americans at all income levels have access to credit cards. (Perhaps too much access?)

Because checks could "bounce", i.e. the holder of funds no longer had a sufficient sum in his account to cover the authorized note (check), sellers became reluctant to allow purchases to be made with checks. That caused the development of the debit card, another form of plastic payment. Unlike credit cards that allows the purchaser some lag time between the time of acquisition of the purchased item and the subsequent bill seeking actual payment, a debit card authorizes the seller to access your bank account at the time of purchase (acquisition). So, when purchasing groceries with a credit card, you walk out of the store with your groceries, but you don't actually pay for them until you get the bill from the credit card company some 20-25 days later. But, if you purchase your groceries with a debit card, your bank account is accessed and you have paid for the groceries just moments before you walk out with your bags. Next to cold, hard cash, retailers prefer debit cards to checks—even to credit cards, for which retailers must pay a fee to the credit card company itself.

EFT (Electronic Funds Transfer): *is a money consisting of technology based authorizations.*

And, the latest money innovation is the EFT (electronic fund transfer). If you have learned to pay some of your bills online, or if you are paid by your employer via direct deposit, you are using EFT's. An electronic fund transfer is merely a pre-determined authorization that allows Bank A to withdraw funds from a specified account held at its facilities and transfer those funds to Bank B which will deposit the sum into an account held at its facilities. So, if you are paid via direct deposit, your employer sends a document to its bank that cites its bank account, and then lists various employees (probably by Social Security number), the sums each is to be paid, and to what bank (and bank account number) each employee wants his/her compensation directed. Your employer's bank makes one large withdrawal (debit) from your employer's account, and sends individual sums to the various banks designated by various employees. At your bank, your account is credited (a deposit is made into your account). So, ultimately, EFT's simply require authorization paperwork, and then banks just "talk" to one another on payday.

While EFT's do not (yet) comprise a large percentage of our economic transactions, EFT transactions are some of the largest when they do occur. And, as Americans get more and more comfortable with technology and computers, America is headed for a currency-free economy.

To summarize, as societies progress and confidence levels are established, the forms of money evolve. Metal coins are as old as recorded history, and we have used commodities, paper, plastic, and now computer transmitted digits. Only coins and currency are legal tender; all other forms are voluntary. But, as confidence builds, most of the forms are used routinely.

Standard of Value and Store of Value

Developing a currency form of money does generate two significant benefits: 1) standard of value, and 2) store of value.

A currency allows all products and services to be valued as increments of some established unit. In the United States, the standard of value is one dollar, so all goods and services are valued as multiples or fractions of one buck. The reason the trapper and the store clerk (in the previous section) might have trouble negotiating a deal is because they might not be able to agree on the value of a particular fur or a sack of flour. But, with the creation of a currency, the trapper can seek to convert his furs into as much currency as he can get (depending upon their size, quality, scarcity, and so on), and the store clerk can put a price tag on each item he sells. The fur trader might still disagree with the seller's price tag, but at least the goods will be measurable to a common standard. So, the trapper can get currency from the buyer of furs, skins, and hides, and then he can walk into the general store with an idea of how much currency might be needed to acquire his desired items. Again, price tags are not written in stone – perhaps some haggling will occur – but any transaction will be easier to facilitate one way or another because both parties have started from a place of a common standard.

Standard of Value: regards the use of money to measure the worth of produced goods and services.

Currency also stores value much better than commodity money. If gems (diamonds or pearls) or metals (gold or silver) are used, the amount of value can change if the gem gets cracked or the coin gets marred. (Indeed, some medieval kings would cheat their subjects by filing indents around the edges of coins, thereby shaving metal to make more coins; but the value of each coin was actually lower than it should have been.) Unless a dollar bill is torn or disfigured and needs to be replaced, a bill can be used over and over for years. Whether right off the printing press or wrinkled and faded from years of use, a one dollar bill will be have the same face value.

Store of Value: regards a money's ability to keep its value stable.

MEASUREMENTS of OUR MONEY SUPPLY

We will later learn that a general strategy to pursuing our major economic goals and/or addressing our twin economic problems (inflation and unemployment) involves controlling the country's money supply. But, control really only means either increasing or decreasing the supply, so in order to decide which of the options to undertake, one must first know how big the money supply is.

In the early 1970's, our country used three designations to measure the country's money supply, M-1, M-2, and M-3. These broad categories differed according to the liquidity of the forms of money and assets contained in the designations. In 2006, the Federal Reserve's Board of Governors decided to reduce the country's money designations from three to two; we now simply use M-1 and M-2.

M-1 is the measurement of money that consists of coins and currency, i.e. cash, and checking accounts. Money orders and travelers checks are also part of this category. The point of this category is that these forms of money are highly accessible and spendable. The cash in your wallet or pocketbook is easily accessible, and the funds in the checkbook are expected to be spent soon.

M-2 is the designation that adds savings accounts and investments that tie up funds for a short period of time, usually one year or less. Money market accounts and mutual fund accounts are common examples of such "short term" investment assets. Funds are accessible, but there may be a bit of time lag between one's request of funds and actually receiving the funds.

As the chart below shows, the M-1 portion of our money supply in 2008 was about $1.4 trillion (over half of which was currency), and savings accounts plus time deposits under $100,000 pushed the M-2 total to $7.7 trillion.

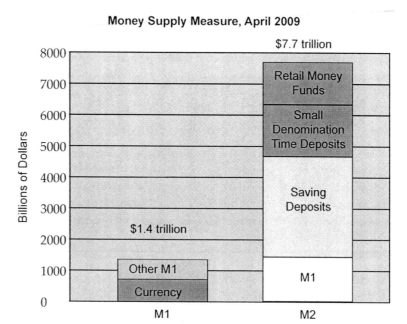

Money Supply Measure, April 2009

M-2 is the designation that is most commonly used to measure the country's money supply.

Quantity Theory of Money

If we change the supply of money in the country, what will happen? Would increasing the money supply be good? Would decreasing the money supply be good? The answer to those questions depends upon existing economic conditions, but it is rather clear that changing the supply of money in the economy can have a significant impact of price levels and business output.

Classical economists advocate a relationship between the money supply and the general economy called the Quantity Theory of Money which is expressed in the equation

$$M \text{ times } V = P \text{ times } Q$$

where,

M = the total money supply

V = the velocity of money, that is, the average number of times per year that a dollar is used to make a purchase of a final good or services; velocity can be calculated by dividing the total output of the economy by the money supply

P = price level (the average price of a transaction)

Q = total quantity (the number of goods and services produced and sold)

The left hand side of the equation focuses on the value of consumer spending, and the right side focuses on the value gained by suppliers. So, the theory says that the value of purchases (PQ) in the economy must be equal to the money supply multiplied by the number of times money changes hands (MV).

Ok. Fine. But, just what are we to make of that? Boiled down to its essence, the classical economists asserted that the price level of the economy was due to the amount of money circulating in the economy. If we alter the equation to isolate P, we get:

$$P = \frac{MV}{Q}$$

And, let's use an example to illustrate the theory's point If the money supply (M) is assumed to be $100, velocity is 10, and output is 50, then

$$P = \frac{100 \times 10}{50} = \frac{1,000}{50} = 20$$

The general price level is $20.

But, if the velocity and output remain as they were, what happens to the price level if the money supply is increased by 50% to $150? Then,

$$P = \frac{150 \times 10}{50} = \frac{1,500}{50} = \$30$$

So, now the price level also rises by 50% from $20 to $30

Hence, says the Quantity Theory of Money advocates, changing the money supply impacts the price levels, i.e. if the government increases the money supply, it will only cause prices to rise.

Well, maybe. The Quantity Theory of Money is based upon two major assumptions. First, its fans assume that the economy is rather steady and is already functioning at full capacity, i.e. full employment and full production. The other assumption is that the velocity of money is also rather constant; people's spending habits are routine and stable over time. Hence, if all resources are being used in an economy and the economy is at full productive potential, then consumers and businesses will simply use any additional money in the money supply to bid up prices on the available goods and services.

However, if an economy is operating at less than full potential, then increasing the money supply can increase output and not necessarily cause a rise in prices or only a modest increase. And, modern economists also challenge the notion that velocity is stable. Data shows that people save much more or save much less at different periods, and such saving/

spending habits can have significant impacts on output and/or price levels, depending upon existing economic conditions. Levels of interest rates can alter consumers' spending habits, and concerns about future price expectations (e.g. inflation) can change spending patterns.

The Quantity Theory of Money reminds us that tinkering with the money supply should be done with great care. Sometimes, changes in the money supply can facilitate growth in production and employment, but at other times it will lead to increased prices. As is so often the case in economics, it all depends on what the existing economic conditions are.

Consumer Price Index and Real Value of Money

Consumer Price Index: is a measurement of a money's reflective value over time.

In a capitalistic economic system, prices are allowed to fluctuate, and indeed prices on all sorts of goods and services change all the time. The price increases or decreases of individual products don't matter very much, but the general level of prices in the country does. So, in order to measure such aggregate price movements, economists use a series of indexes, and the one that deserves our attention is called the Consumer Price Index, or the CPI.

An index is merely a comparison of two prices at different points in time, and the Consumer Price Index is a comparison of the cost of a typical market basket of goods in a specific year versus the cost of that same basket of goods in another year. Using food and beverages, housing, clothing, transportation, medical care, and other basic living items as the elements in the basket, the Bureau of Labor Statistics (part of the U.S. Department of Labor) calculates the annual indexes.

Below is a chart of selected Consumer Price Indexes from 1913 (when the government began calculating the CPI) to available 2010 data; 1982 is considered the base year, so these numbers indicate how price levels have risen compared to the base year. Hence, for example, the CPI of 174 in December of 2000 indicates that prices increased 74% since 1982, and the CPI of 216.7 in January 2010 indicates that prices rose 116.7% since 1982.

Clearly, if one's income remains pretty much the same, but price levels rise, the ability to afford the purchases you are accustomed to making is impaired. Your *purchasing power* has declined; because prices have risen, you cannot buy as many items as before. In order to be able to acquire the same items as you did before prices rose, you need to acquire more income. And, indeed, the CPI is often used by employees or employee unions to seek raises so as to keep up with the rising prices. Every so often (sometimes annually) the federal government increases Social Security sums paid to eligible seniors to help maintain the value of the Social Security benefit paid to a recipient, and Cost of Living Adjustments (COLA's) are triggered in negotiated labor contracts.

Year	Jan	Feb	Mar	Apr	May	Jun	Jul	Aug	Sep	Oct	Nov	Dec
Consumer Price Index History 1982-84 = 100												
1913	9.8	9.8	9.8 9.	8 9.7	9.8	9.9	9.9	10.0	10.0	10.1	10.0	
1920	19.3	19.5	19.7	20.3	20.6	20.9	20.8	20.3	20.0	19.9	19.8	19.4
1930	17.1	17.0	16.9	17.0	16.9	16.8	16.6	16.5	16.6	16.5	16.4	16.1
1940	13.9	14.0	14.0	14.0	14.0	14.1	14.0	14.0	14.0	14.0	14.0	14.1
1950	23.5	23.5	23.6	23.6	23.7	23.8	24.1	24.3	24.4	24.6	24.7	25.0
1960	29.3	29.4	29.4	29.5	29.5	29.6	29.6	29.6	29.6	29.8	29.8	29.8
1970	37.8	38.0	38.2	38.5	38.6	38.8	39.0	39.0	39.2	39.4	39.6	39.8
1980	77.8	78.9	80.1	81.0	81.8	82.7	82.7	83.3	84.0	84.8	85.5	86.3
1990	127.4	128.0	128.7	128.9	129.2	129.9	130.4	131.6	132.7	133.5	133.8	133.8
2000	168.8	169.8	171.2	171.3	171.5	172.4	172.8	172.8	173.7	174.0	174.1	174.0
2010	216.7	217.7	217.6	218.0	218.2	217.9	218.0	218.3	218.4			

Source: Bureau of Labor Statistics (2010)

Caution must be exercised as such wage increases, to keep up with rising prices, can in turn just cause **pressures for more price hikes, i.e. a self-perpetuating spiral begins to develop,** but the Consumer Price Index nevertheless provides a useful attempt to measure changes in price levels over selected periods of time.

CHAPTER SUMMARY

In a very real sense, money is arbitrary. While its purpose is always the same, to facilitate transactions (or store wealth while awaiting future transaction facilitation), the actual form of money can be whatever people agree to make it. A "good" money form is one that is durable and transportable, and the benefits of an established money are that it can store value and help provide a standard against which the value of various goods and services are measured. Forms have evolved throughout history, metal coins being the most prominent. But, the modern era has relied on paper (currency and check), plastic (credit cards and debit cards), and now EFTs (electronic fund transfers). Indeed, we are very close to a currency-free economy.

Since economic growth is probably the economic goal in our economic system, and we measure that growth, that economic activity with a concept called GDP (Gross Domestic Product), our economy needs a way to measure the amount of money in our money supply. There are multiple measures for our money supply, but the most common measurement is M1 that measures the liquid forms of money in our economy, i.e. cash on hand, checking accounts, money orders, and traveler's checks, i.e. forms of money that are easily and quickly spent.

Because inflation can occur, the purchasing power (real value) of money can change, and the Consumer Price Index (CPI) is the measurement used to determine the nominal versus the real value of money over time.

▶▶| *Chapter 9 Review*

Key concepts are:

1. Money is a medium of exchange that is "created" to make transactions easier to achieve. Barter regards two parties attempting to "make a trade" without the use of any money, but such transactions can be both cumbersome and inequitable, so money can make trades occur faster and more fairly.

2. The form of money can be whatever parties agree to make it: historical examples include metal coins, gems, animal hides, shells, beads, printed paper, checks, credit/debit cards, and EFT's. But, money also include items such as paper clips or buttons – as long as parties voluntarily agreed to it.

3. There are at least two benefits to modern forms of money: a) standard of value, and b) store of value.

4. Money is measured according to its liquidity; M1 is the most liquid and the measurement most often used by federal authorities when reporting the size of the U.S. money supply.

5. The Quantity Theory of Money is a theory that asserts an increase (or decrease) in the money supply will cause an increase (or decrease) the general price level of products in the country.

6. The value, or purchasing power, of money changes over time, and the Consumer Price Index is a measurement to indicate those fluctuations.

Key terms:

money, barter, fiat money, legal tender, EFT, standard of value, store of value, M1, Quantity Theory of Money, Consumer Price Index

CHAPTER 10

BANKING AND THE FEDERAL RESERVE SYSTEM

We learned in earlier chapters that there are "main players" in our economy's Circular Flow of Activity, namely consumers (households), businesses, and government. We discussed the need for balance between leakages (savings, taxes, and imports) and injections (loans, government spending, and exports), and in the previous chapter we noted that the only purpose of money was to spend it, although one could spend "now" or one could spend "later." We need to add one more main player to our Circular Flow of Activity that facilitates the "saving and "loaning", the place where "later" spending is stored: banks.

BANKING BASICS

Banking Categories

Until 1999, banking in the U.S. was divided into two segments: 1) commercial banking and 2) investment banking. When you hear or read the word "bank," chances are you are thinking about the most traditional enterprise, a commercial bank, which is the most prominent party in the commercial banking category. But, in addition to banks, savings and loan associations (commonly called thrifts) and credit

Commercial Bank: is a traditional bank that loans collected savings to worthy borrowers.

unions also serve as financial intermediaries. Commercial banks seek to attract depositors by offering checking and savings accounts at appealing interest rates, funds for lending to parties. These parties may need to borrow to start a business, expand a business, and so on. In this sense, banks are merely "middle men" or "brokers," offering individuals a safe place to store their extra income while simultaneously creating a pool of funds that qualified borrowers can access for risk-acceptable purposes. Some of the top commercial banks in 2012 include Citibank, Bank of America, JP Morgan, Wachovia, Wells Fargo, HSBC, and Suntrust.

Investment Bank: is a fiduciary that buys stocks, bonds, and real estate for its depositors, and investors.

Thrifts (savings and loans institutions) once played a larger role in our history, but they still represent the second largest category. They, too, serve as a place for some parties to save funds, but their focus is on loans regarding real estate, e.g. building or buying a home.

A third category is the credit union, a financial institution formed by people (members) who have some sort of common bond. Employees of the same profession may band together and create a credit union where people in that profession may deposit their extra income and later seek a loan for buying a car, taking a vacation, remodeling a kitchen, and so on. Because one is a "member" of the financial organization, it may be easier to be accepted for a loan.

The second segment of banking is called investment banking. Prior to 1999 and the passage of the Financial Services Modernization Act, commercial banking and investment banking were separated.

Thrift Bank: is a bank that specializes in real estate loans.

Commercial banking, the more traditional banking, was highly regulated to protect consumers' savings, but investment banks don't accept deposits. But, investment banking serves a couple of different purposes which, in the minds of government officials, don't require the same scrutiny. One service that investment banking provides is assistance with business mergers and acquisitions. Corporations merge

Credit Union: is a member owned fidu-ciary based upon a com-monality (e.g., same profession).

with or buy out one another with regularity, but neutral advice is often sought and assistance is needed for stocks to be valued, offers to be tendered, records to be kept, and so on, and outside parties, investment banks, provide that supervisory and managerial help.

The second, more controversial, service regards actual investments. These banks attract "depositors," investors who place large sums in the hands of these banks. These banks then invest in a variety of more complicated securities with names such as derivatives (collateralized debt obligations), credit default swaps, and auction-rate preferred securities. Sometimes the banks themselves will create the investment opportunity and solicit wealthy parties to invest, and sometimes the banks will simply act as a broker between investors (e.g.,a pension fund) and a borrower (corporation) and charge a fee. The top investment banks in 2012 were Bank of America, Barclays, Citigroup, Credit Suisse, Deutsche Bank, Goldman Sachs, JP Morgan Chase, Morgan Stanley, and USB.

HISTORY of BANKING

One of the primary purposes of a bank is to provide stability in the liquidity of commerce and entrepreneurial risk-taking, and that rather essentially means that banks, even efficient and ethical ones, will acquire a great deal of influence, if not power. Hence, it should not surprise anyone to realize that economics, especially banking, and politics are often intertwined, and we need to recall a bit our political history when reviewing the history of banking in the U.S.

We often forget that the Revolutionary War (The War for Independence) was a lengthy one; it started in 1775 (before our Declaration of Independence on July 4, 1776) and didn't end until 1783. The Second Continental Congress indeed met to declare our independence in the Philadelphia summer heat in 1776. However, the beginnings of the federal government didn't occur until 1786 with the Articles of Confederation. We soon realized that the Articles were too weak and subsequently drafted the U.S. Constitution in 1787. Although it was completed on September 17, 1787, it was not sufficiently ratified until June of 1788 (New Hampshire's approval provided the required 2/3rds even though all 13 states would eventually ratify), The federal government did not actually begin operations until March 4, 1889.

Much of our history regarding banking is a story about the constraint of power. Banks are required to be authorized (chartered) by a government, and colonies and states had authorized banks for years. Wealthy individuals pooled their funds to start a bank that, in turn, loaned funds to businesses and farmers. While loans became the lifeblood of commerce, city bankers usually made only short term loans (3-6 months) to businesses who would buy supplies and pay employees to facilitate sales. Out of these sales, loans plus interest, would be repaid, but rural banks were willing to make year long loans to farmers who battled the seasons. Since loans were made in the form of a paper money, these banks needed to first create money for use in the local economies, and banks printed "colonial script" during the decades that led up to the Revolutionary War. (Once the bankers in Great Britain learned of the practice, they convinced Parliament to pass a law outlawing such a practice, which added fuel to the colonists' desire to free themselves from British rule).

But, once the country opted to wage war for independence, it created a large debt to businesses who provided war supplies as well as to the soldiers themselves, and, while states had created state-chartered banks (The Bank of Pennsylvania founded in 1780, for example), the first United States Bank was created in 1791. However, this creation occurred only after a major philosophical feud between Thomas Jefferson and the political party known then as the Jeffersonian Democrats, and Alexander Hamilton and the other major political party called the Federalists. This debate continues to today.

Thomas Jefferson, a farmer and rural landowner, was not a fan of cities, commerce, and speculators. He was fearful of concentrated power and distrusted banks. Additionally, he argued that since the Constitution did not articulate any power to the federal government for such an action, he contended any banking authority belonged to the states. He vehemently opposed the creation of a national bank. Alexander Hamilton, on the other hand, grew up in the banking business and saw no reason to fear a well-crafted institution. He argued that the country needed a strong central financial institution to guard the country's money supply, and to lend money to private banks when liquidity problems occurred. He also contended that since the Constitution granted the national government the right to levy taxes and borrow money, the federal government had an implied power to create a national bank if it needed to do so.

The Federalists won the initial debate, but when the national bank's charter expired in 1811, it was not renewed. After the War of 1812, President James Madison persuaded Congress to charter a second national bank in 1816. However, its charter was also not renewed when it ended in 1836. And, the U.S. had no central bank again for decades. State governments became more prominent in chartering and regulating private banks.

The bulk of banking history between the 1830's and 1930's concerns state supervision – or lack of it – as private banks began to proliferate throughout the United States. From 1837 to 1863, the only banks in the country were state-chartered ones; some estimates suggest that there 10,000 private banks in the U.S., with nearly as many currencies. Counterfeiting became a significant problem. In an attempt to control and stabilize currencies that had been created by various private banks, President Lincoln and Congress passed the National Bank Act that authorized a few private national banks to "loan" the federal government money by buying government-backed securities (bonds, i.e. IOU's). The government would in turn issue these banks the equivalent in national bank notes, the new federal currency printed by the Office of the Comptroller. The new act also established a national Comptroller who was authorized to regulate and inspect all banks, and the new legislation placed a 10% tax on the currency of any state-chartered bank (which essentially forced all banks to utilize the new national currency). These national notes became the country's currency until the creation of the Federal Reserve System some 50 years later.

Still, while the Constitution allows the federal government to create a money supply, it doesn't seem to allow the United States to create a national bank. So, with all of the historical ebb and flow, America did not have a true central bank.

The second half of the 19th century saw American free enterprise grow significantly, which facilitated a growing standard of living. This, in turn, facilitated a growing population. Immigration also helped. This self-perpetuating cycle of successful entrepreneurialism, increasing standard of living, and growing population caused a need for increased banking services to keep up, and indeed they did. Before the financial crisis of 1929, some 30,000 banks offered checking account and loan services all across America. Most banking operations were local. Banks accepted savings from local citizens and made loans to local parties. And, since loans were usually straightforward and simple (and highly collateralized), there were few bank failures.

In 1913 the Federal Reserve System was created. The Fed consists of 12 regional banks (discussed in more detail in a later chapter), but it has essentially brought the nation's private banks under control. In 1933, the Federal Deposit Insurance Corporation was created. The FDIC protects depositors in the event of a bank failure (originally up to $100,000, but recently increased to $250,000, per account). Congress has instituted a variety of regulations to protect the solvency of our banking system. Some of those regulations were later repealed; some were alleged to have contributed to the financial meltdown of 2007-2008. Political debates are ongoing regarding what governmental supervision of financial institutions is now appropriate.

HOW DO BANKS WORK?

In ancient times, warehouses and temples served as banks, though the only service that the bank provided was safe storage. Farmers who experienced an exceptionally good harvest would store their excess produce for later use, and wealthy individuals would sometimes store precious jewels and metals in such secure places. Hence, the original banks merely offered a safe place to store valuable items until they were needed at a later date. Customers paid the bank owner a fee for providing the secure location.

But, banks are capable of much more, and the banking service is truly a community service. In their essence, banks serve as brokers between those who have extra and those who wish to have more; in this case, the "extra" and the "wish to have more" means money (cash). Recall that the function of money is to spend it. Spend it now or spend it later; the question is not whether you will spend your money, but *when* you will spend your money. Should you have more money in your possession than you presently need to spend, what do you do with the extra? Where do you put your savings? Some will save money in a jar, a coffee can, under the mattress, in a box in the closet, or buried in the back yard. There's nothing exactly wrong with such a strategy – except that the funds are not especially stored in a safe place. One is relying on secrecy for safety. But, if you are ever spotted accessing the funds, the safety is gone.

A bank, a private business, can be started to offer members of the community a safer, more secure environment in which to place their extra income and assets. To entice potential customers to place their extra income and assets with the bank, the bank offers to pay interest on such deposits. So, instead of using a risky hiding place that pays no interest, individuals can use a private business that provides safes and vaults and alarms – and income (interest) payments.

Why would a bank pay people to save their money with it? Because the profit side of the banking business lies in the loans that a bank can make with the funds on deposit in it. Various parties have needs to acquire extra funds and would hope to borrow. Parents need to get Jimmy's teeth fixed, homeowners need to remodel the kitchen, families wish to buy a new car, and young couples want to take a special vacation. Existing businesses need to cover cash flow shortages, stock up on seasonal inventory, expand the warehouse, replace worn out equipment, or explore new locations. And, would-be entrepreneurs need start-up funds to begin their dream ventures.

So, banks act as the middle man between those with "extra" and those who are looking for "more." Of course, banks will assess the risks associated with parties who wish to get a loan (not all qualify), but the role of the bank is to pool the idle, extra income and assets of a community and serve as a source for eligible persons to borrow the funds and put them to work in the local economy. The leakage of savings is injected back into the circular flow in the form of loans. And, the bank makes money because the interest it charges the borrowers is higher than the interest it pays to its depositors.

There are four major functions banks perform. First, banks provide lending services. While individually desirable, saved funds are withdrawn from the community's local circular flow of activity, which then limits potential production, employment, and economic growth. So, banks can serve as a mechanism to funnel funds back into the community, facilitating the achievement of worthy needs. Borrowing entails risk, so banks offer some professionalism in assessing such risks and accepting/denying loan requests, and charging interest rate fees accordingly. The higher the risk, the higher the interest rate.

Second, banks provide investment products called securities. Since depositors can quickly access funds in checking and savings accounts, banks won't offer much interest for such accounts, but banks can offer other investment products that pay higher rates of interest to customers who are willing to commit their funds for long(er) periods of time. An example of such security products is a certificate of deposit.

Asset management services is a third category. Wealthy individuals, or individuals for whom a trust has been established (usually because one is too young or too old), may have their assets monitored and/or invested by banking professionals for a fee.

The fourth function a bank (an investment bank) provides is assistance with business mergers and acquisitions, or assistance with a corporation issuing stock to the public.

The MULTIPLIER EFFECT

One last foundational concept regarding bank operations is called the Multiplier Effect. In their capacity to provide loans, banks actually influence the money supply in the country. Here's how that works.

Multiplier Effect: regards the impact of savings, and loans on the money supply.

I live in Florida, so let's assume that, after the orange crop is harvested, farmers were able to accumulate savings of $1,000,000.00 They could keep the funds under the mattresses in their bedrooms, in coffee cans in their attics, or in a local bank. They chose the bank since the bank has a nice, secure safe, and they can earn some interest when deposited in the bank.

But, of course, a major function of a bank is to loan funds to worthy purposes, turning leakages into injections. With a legal reserve requirement, not all of the deposited savings can be loaned. We'll assume a 10% reserve requirement, so $100,000 must be set aside (for daily operations such as customer withdrawals), but $900,000 is available for loans.

Let's assume that a local entrepreneur has a sound business idea to build a new orange juice processor, so the bank loans him $900,000 which he uses to hire a contractor to construct a building and buy some processing equipment. The contractor and the equipment company take the entrepreneur's funds to pay their employees.

The employees opt to deposit their paychecks into the bank, so $900,000 winds up being deposited back into the bank. But, again, the bank sets aside 10%, or $90,000, and can subsequently loan out $810,000 to a local orange grower who wants to expand its warehouse to store picked produce..

The orange grower uses its $810,000 to hire another local contractor to build the expansion; the contractor pays its employees, and the $810,000 comes back to the banking system again, only to be loaned out (minus the fractional reserve) again – and again – and again.

So, we could illustrate this "creation" of money thusly,

	Deposits	Set Aside Amount	Loanable Amount
Initial:	1,000,000.00	100,000.00	900,000.00
New:	900,000.00	90,000.00	810,000.00
New	810,000.00	81,000.00	729,000.00
New	729,000.00	72,900.00	656,100.00
New	656,100.00	65,610.00	590,490.00
New:	590,490.00	59,049.00	531,441.00
New	531,441.00	53,144.10	478,296.90

and so on ....

Total deposits: $10,000,000.00

If all of the funds that were deposited were, in turn, loaned back into the community's circular flow of activity, the bank will have turned the initial $1,000,000.00 into a total sum of $10,000,000.00. The initial deposit of $1 million grew ten-fold to $10 million. Indeed, one can estimate the impact of the multiplier effect with the "formula":

$$\text{Multiplier Effect} = \frac{1}{\text{Legal reserve requirement}}$$

Hence, in our example, $1/10\% = 1/.10 = 10$. If the legal reserve requirement was only 5%, the Multiplier Effect would be $1/.05$, or 20. Or, if the legal reserve requirement was 20%, the Multiplier Effect would be $1/.20$, or 5. Clearly, the percentage of deposits that banks must set aside (not loan) has a significant influence on the amount of money a bank can "create" via the Multiplier Effect.

JUST HOW DOES the FEDERAL RESERVE SYSTEM WORK?

The FED: is America's "Central" bank.

I'm glad you asked that question because that explanation is how we should end this chapter. The Federal Reserve System, established in 1913 and now commonly called The Fed, is essentially the country's national bank and serves as a banker's bank. Actually, The Fed is comprised of 12 individually chartered banks that are scattered across the country, one each in twelve separate districts, and "branch" FED banks exist in most of the districts. Figure 10-1 below shows these districts, the 12 Federal Reserve Bank sites and the 25 branch bank locations.

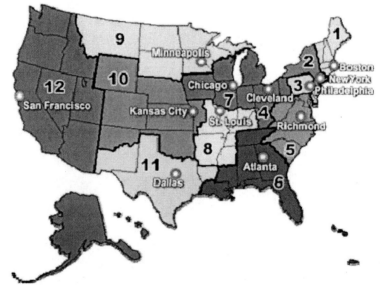

Figure 10-1:

District	Main Bank Location	Branch Location(s)
1	Boston	-
2	New York	Buffalo
3	Philadelphia	-
4	Cleveland	Cincinnati; Pittsburgh
5	Richmond	Baltimore; Charlotte
6	Atlanta	Birmingham; Jacksonville; Nashville; New Orleans
7	Chicago	Detroit
8	St. Louis	Little Rock; Louisville; Memphis
9	Minneapolis	Helena
10	Kansas City	Denver; Oklahoma City; Omaha
11	Dallas	El Paso; Houston; San Antonio
12	San Francisco	Los Angeles; Salt Lake City; Portland; Seattle

(San Francisco office services Hawaii; Seattle office services Alaska)

The Federal Reserve System is controlled by a Board of Directors, called the Board of Governors, which consists of 7 individuals who are appointed by the U.S. President to serve 14 year terms in a staggered fashion. (A member usually serves but 1 term.) In addition to the Board of Governors, the Fed Chairman is also appointed by the President and is considered, after the President of the United States, to be the most influential person on domestic affairs. Whenever the Fed Chairman has reason to speak (and he is required to address Congress every other month or so), the world listens. The current Chairman of the Federal Reserve System is Ben Bernanke; he was initially appointed on February 1, 2006 by President Bush and re-appointed by President Obama on January 28, 2010.

Each of the 12 district banks are private corporations, each with a president and a nine-member board of directors, and each branch bank has its own board of directors. Six of the nine board members are elected by the banks in each district that opt to be member banks of the Federal Reserve System, and the other three board members are designated by the Board of Governors.

The role of the Board of Governors, lead by the Chairman, is to affect *monetary policy*,; i.e., control the nation's money supply. If the country's money supply is increased or decreased, policy objectives can be pursued or achieved, and it is the presumed expertise of the board and chairman to know whether to raise or lower the supply, and by how much. Hardly an easy task.

FED's Purpose

Monetary Policy: regards the FED's attempt to control the nation's money supply.

Our economic system has historically embraced three fundamental economic goals. Additional goals have "come and gone" with our evolving culture and standard of living (e.g. balanced budgets and pollution control), but three have consistently served as the solid foundation of our economy for decades: 1) economic growth, 2) price stability, and 3) full employment. And, our economic system uses two "big picture" strategies to pursue these goals. One is called fiscal policy (to be reviewed in the next chapter) and the other is called *monetary policy.*

Monetary policy is the government's attempt to "control" the nation's money supply because appropriately increasing or decreasing the amount of money in the country can have a major impact on the achievement of our economic goals.

You may recall from the previous chapters on banking that America's history was cluttered with bank panics, recessions, and an array of financial crises. After a significant financial turmoil in 1907, Congress had had enough and created a "national bank", albeit a private one full of checks and balances. The major purpose of the Fed was to prevent bank panics and to create some stability (and thereby credibility) in the U.S. economy.

FED's Tools

The Federal Reserve board has three major tools in its arsenal to affect the nation's money supply:

- Adjustments to the legal reserve requirement
- Adjustments to the discount rate
- Open Market Transactions

Legal Reserve Requirement:

Legal Reserve Requirement: regards a bank's restriction on loanable funds.

Recall that the role of banks, especially traditional, commercial banks, is to create injections out of leakages. When money is saved (deposited into a bank), it is leaked from the economy's circular flow and cannot be used to facilitate transactions that grow the economy and cause jobs. So, banks seek to inject those funds back into circulation via loans. (Whether banks are making sound loans is a separate question, but banks help collect "excess funds" from individuals (savings), and then re-route those funds back into the economy by making loans to parties who wish to address a variety of family or business needs.) But, would it not seem surprising (aggravating?) to you if you walked into your bank one day, asked to make a withdrawal from your account, and the teller said, "Sorry, we don't have any money in the bank today; we loaned it all out. Yes, you do indeed have an account here with us, but we can't give any of your money to you because all of our customers' funds are loaned to various parties at this time. Perhaps some of the borrowers will make a payment later today so that we might have some funds available for you and other customers tomorrow." You might have a few choice words for the teller and the bank.

But, except for historical "bank runs" (that are now a thing of the past due to the creation of the FDIC), such a scenario does not happen. Why not? Because banks cannot loan out all of the funds on deposit with it. Banks are required to hold back a portion of the savings on deposit. They face a legally required percentage to be held in reserve for daily transactions such as withdrawals or even account closures.

Such a legal reserve requirement, then, has a significant impact on the amount of money a bank can loan out, which in turn has an impact on the country's money supply. If the legal reserve requirement is low, say 5%, then banks have the opportunity (assuming parties wish to borrow) to loan out more and the nation's money supply is larger. If the legal reserve requirement is higher, say 15%, then of course, banks must keep more funds on hand, loan out less, and the money supply is therefore more restricted.

Discount Rate:

We said earlier that the Fed, a collection of banks, served as a "banker's bank," and indeed the Fed can loan funds to a member bank in its district. Suppose a local bank, fully in compliance with the legal reserve requirement, and fortunate enough to find acceptable borrowers, began to notice that a larger number of customer withdrawals and/or account closures were occurring. The bank's managers might become concerned that the bank was dangerously low on funds for daily operations. This bank needs a loan to handle its unexpected cash flow challenges. Banks can and do borrow from one another, but banks can also borrow from its district's Fed bank (or branch bank). Our local bank makes a phone call, negotiates acceptable arrangements, and the Fed loans the local bank the amount needed (e.g. via EFT). So, the discount rate is nothing more than an interest rate that the Fed charges for loaning money to member banks.

Discount Rate: is the interest and rate the FED charges bankers.

Why is the tool called a discount rate rather than just simply an interest rate? Technically, the tool is an interest rate, but the Fed collects its payment a bit differently. When you or I borrow say $1,000 at 10% interest, we will ultimately pay $1,100; repay the borrowed $1,000 plus an additional $100 in interest expense. But, if the Fed loans $1,000 to a local bank at 10% interest, the Fed takes its interest payment right off the top and loans the bank only $900. The local bank will need to repay $1,000, but it got only $900, since the loan was discounted.

Just think of the discount rate tool as an interest rate. And, since an interest rate is actually the price tag of money, one can "purchase" money if one is willing to pay the price, the rate interest. We know that demand will go up and down as the price goes up and down. Thus, if the Fed increases its rate, banks will be less inclined to borrow, and the money supply will thereby be less; conversely, if the Fed is willing to lower its interest rate (discount rate), then banks will find it easier to borrow and the money supply can be subsequently larger.

From a practical standpoint, this strategy is rarely used since banks usually borrow from one another rather than directly from the Fed. But, the discount rate serves as the barometer for all other interest rates in the country.

Open Market Transactions:

Open Market Transactions: *regards the FED buying and selling bonds.*

The real action of the Fed occurs in the Federal Open Market Committee. This committee meets eight times a year to supervise open market operations, the main tool used to set monetary policy. This committee has 12 members consisting of the seven members of the Board of Governors, the president of the federal reserve bank in New York, and four other presidents from the other eleven federal reserve banks.

The "action" regards the buying and selling of U.S. Treasury securities (e.g. U.S. Savings bonds). Bonds are nothing more than I.O.U.s; you loan a party some money, and the party gives you a document that promises to repay the borrowed sum plus a stipulated interest amount on a specified day in the future. So, when you buy a U.S. Savings bond, you are loaning the government money and the U.S. government will repay you according to the terms cited on the certificate (the bond). Bonds can be printed to look quite prestigious and impressive, and there are important legal agreements to be made clear, but a bond is really just a simple transaction. Private businesses as well as all levels of governments can seek to raise funds by selling bonds.

Hence, the U.S. government uses bonds as a way to raise money (in addition to levying taxes or charging fees), and it is up to the investor to decide if the purchase of a U.S. Savings bond is an appropriate investment. What matters to an investor? The amount of interest to be earned, and the likelihood of being repaid matters most. Until recently, the U.S. Savings Bond was considered the safest investment in the world, so the interest rate paid on a government bond was rather low; but repayment was certain. So, the Fed as well as governments have little difficulty in attracting all the investors they want. The interest rate that the Fed or governments must be willing to pay does change from time to time to attract a sufficient number of willing investors.

Who would be interested in purchasing U.S. Savings bonds? Parties that want a safe and consistent, albeit low rate, of return. And, private companies that need to "pay claims" are just the types of parties that need a solid segment in their investment portfolios; think insurance companies and retirement benefit companies. Such companies receive premiums or account payments by individual customers, and the companies invest those sums to be able to earn the funds that are used to pay out claims as needed. These companies will also make riskier investments to earn higher returns, but every sound portfolio also needs a segment that invests in stable, solid, "count on it" opportunities. U.S. Savings bonds fit that bill.

Hence, the FED will buy and sell federal securities. It works through securities dealers and, prompted by the decisions of the Federal Open Market Committee, transactions are carried out by the Domestic Trading Desk of the Federal Reserve Bank of New York Not surprisingly, besides seeking to impact the actual money supply, such buying and selling of bonds and other securities will also affect the federal funds rate, the rate banks charge when borrowing from one another. The effects will be discussed in more detail in a later chapter, but suffice it to say here that the Fed will decrease the money supply by selling bonds and it will increase the money supply when it buys securities.

CHAPTER SUMMARY

While banking performs an essential function in our economic circular flow of activity (turns leakages into injections), America's history is one of suspicion of banking and its power. America reluctantly began its country with a national bank, but then opted to operate without one for nearly 100 years before creating the Federal Reserve Bank System in 1913. Banks originally were formed to receive depositors' savings and subsequently provide loans to low risk borrowers, a function that has always been highly regulated, but some of America's largest, current banks are also investment banks that engage in activities that have not been regulated.

The Federal Reserve System seeks to monitor and control the nation's money supply to prevent inflation and/or facilitate economic growth. It uses three tools to influence the country's money supply: 1) adjusting the legal reserve requirement, 2) adjusting the discount rate, and 3) buying/selling bonds

▶▶| *Chapter 10 Review*

Key concepts

1. The primary purpose of banks is to re-route savings back into the economy's circular flow, i.e. turn leakages into injections

2. The four types of banks are commercial banks, investment banks, savings & loans, and credit unions.

3. While the U.S. has always chartered state banks, the U.S. has been historically reluctant to create a national bank.

4. Banks perform four basic functions: a) lending services, 2) investment services, 3) estate/asset management, and 4) mergers and acquisitions.

5. The Multiplier Effect indicates the "rippling" impact of a deposit on the nation's money supply.

6. The Federal Reserve System, created in 1913, is a series of banks that are designed to monitor and control the country's money supply

7. The Federal Reserve System has three tools to influence the money supply: 1) legal reserve requirement, 2) discount rate, and 3) buying and selling bonds

Key terms

commercial bank, investment bank, thrift, credit union, Multiplier Effect, monetary policy, Federal Reserve System, legal reserve requirement, discount rate, open market transactions

CHAPTER
11

FISCAL POLICY AND TAX STRATEGIES

Chapter 10 indicated that our economic system embraces three foundational economic goals – economic growth, price stability, and "full" employment – and adds additional goals from time to time as circumstances seem to require. But, these virtuous goals are not achieved by accident or luck. Governments use a couple of strategies to promote these goals and/or resolve the problems associated with not achieving them, and *fiscal policy* is one of those two strategies. (Monetary policy is the other which was described in the previous chapter.)

WHAT IS FISCAL POLICY?

Fiscal policy is the government's right to tax and spend. For the U.S. federal government, Article 1, Section 8 of the Constitution says, "The Congress shall have Power To lay and collect Taxes, Duties, Imposts, and Excises, to pay the Debts and provide for the common Defence and general Welfare of the United States..." And, because some controversy developed over the next century regarding whether the wording of Section 8 allowed for an income tax and if it did, how such a tax could be levied, the Sixteenth Amendment was ratified in 1913 and states, "The Congress shall have power to lay and collect taxes on income, from whatever source derived, without appointment among the several States, and without regard to any census or enumeration." While the issue of what services

Fiscal Policy:
regards the
government's
right to tax
and spend.
and programs government should render, as well as what the size of government should be is a legitimate political debate, once government has opted to provide a service or program to its citizens, it logically follows that revenue must be collected somehow to pay for those efforts.

Private Versus Public Consumption

Economists and public administrators usually reference what is often called the Public Goods and Services Model to determine what products and programs are most appropriately delivered by government, and then which are most efficiently and effectively rendered by private sector businesses. The model groups products and services according to two factors: 1) exclusivity, and 2) consumption. The table below highlights the four groupings that are possible.

	Consumption	
Exclusivity	**Individual**	**Joint**
Yes	Private Goods (e.g. candy bar)	Toll Goods (e.g. amusement park)
No	Common-Pool Goods (e.g. fish in the sea)	Public Goods (e.g. police/fire protection)

Consumption refers to who gains the benefit from the existence of the particular product or service or program. Individual consumption means that the benefit is enjoyed by only 1 person and all others are denied the benefit of consumption of that particular item. If you eat a meal at a local restaurant, you are the only one who enjoys the pleasure of eating those specific food items. Joint consumption, on the other hand, means that the benefits of a particular product or service can be enjoyed by a group of individuals. If you attend a Fourth of July celebration that includes fireworks, you and all other attendees have the same opportunity to enjoy the sights and sounds of the celebration.

Exclusivity regards whether or not there is a high degree of control between a seller and a buyer in a transaction. When you purchase a meal at the local restaurant, your consumption of that meal is quite exclusive; you are the only one who gets to enjoy that delicious piece of fish. However, that fish was likely caught in the ocean or a lake where many fishermen equally enjoyed the opportunity to catch fish. It is not feasible to charge fishermen for using only the sections of water they fished in, but once caught, it is feasible for the fishermen to charge the restaurant who then charges you for the specific fish that was caught and prepared.

So, the model provides four categories or groups of products and services. Private goods are products and services where consumption is done individualistically and it is possible to charge that individual for the exclusive opportunity to enjoy that consumption. Most of the products and services sold in the marketplace fit this category, and this is the area where free enterprise and private sector competition work well.

Toll goods are products where enjoyment can be experienced by multiple individuals at the same time, and where charging a fee to each person on the group is possible. People attending the symphony or visiting the museum can simultaneously enjoy the music or the exhibits, yet each must pay a ticket to enter the location where the enjoyment occurs. This strategy can work well in free enterprise if the product is a theatre, a library, a sports arena, and so on, but some toll goods, such as cable TV or utilities (water or electricity) require governmental regulation to prevent monopolization.

Common-pool goods are items that are enjoyed by each consumer, but there is no feasible way to charge each person for his/her consumption. Again, there is no way to charge a fisherman for the actual water he/she fishes in, we cannot charge for the air we breathe, and so on. Government's role here is one of regulation, if it has a role at all.

But, public goods are called public for a reason; and this is where government plays a large role in our economy. (Government services account for 20-25% of our GDP.) Public services are products and services where joint consumption occurs and it is not possible to charge each consumer for his/her particular slice of consumption. Our national highway system (except the toll roads) and our public safety are two examples of public goods.

What Products/Services Does Government Provide?

Given the background noted above, we know that government should focus primarily on public goods. But, can we be more specific?

Budgets, whether personal or public, are little more than priorities expressed in financial terms, so one need look no further than the respective government budgets to decipher what products, services, and/or programs are of major importance. The matrix below highlights the major services that governments provide, as well as which revenue source each level of government relies on to fund those services and programs.

Primary Public Sector Services and Taxes

Level of Government	Major Programs/Services	Major Tax Source
Federal	Social Security, Medicare, national defense	income
State	education, welfare, state police	sales
Local	public safety, utilities, roads	property

Federal:

With perhaps the exception of the Terrorist Attack on 9/11, the event that has made the most profound impact on the U.S. is the Great Depression. It forever changed the role of the federal government in the country. Washington, D.C. spent about $3.6 trillion (that trillion with a "t") in FY2012, which represents 24% of the expected Gross Domestic Product for that year. The U.S. federal government is the nation's largest employer and is responsible for nearly 1 out of every 4 dollars spent in America.

And, on what did we spend $3.6 trillion? President Obama's budget for FY 2012 can be broken down to essentially 5 sections, of which 4 comprise relatively equal priorities. A bit more than one fifth, i.e. 22% of the federal government's expenses regards the Social Security program. Started in 1935 (during the Great Depression), the Social Security program mainly provides monetary benefits to Americans reaching the age of retirement, although other beneficiaries of the program include surviving spouses and children of deceased workers, as well as Americans who have become disabled. Approximately $775 billion was spent on these services in FY 2012.

Nearly $730 billion, or about 21% of the budget, regards expenditures for Medicare, Medicaid, and CHIP (Children's Health Insurance Program).

Medicare is the health coverage program for the elderly or disabled, Medicaid is the health coverage program for the indigent, and CHIP earmarks health care coverage for the children of low income families.

A third "fifth" of the federal budget regards national defense and related expenses. Some $690 billion, or about 19%, was designated for national security activities, including over $130 billion spent on the wars in Iraq and Afghanistan.

Two other budget sections comprise another fifth of the federal budget for FY 2012. Safety next programs make up about 12% of the expenses, and include programs like Supplemental Security Income (SSI), earned income and child tax credits, food stamps, school meals, foster and adoptive care programs, home energy assistance, and other efforts that aid other needy populations.

The other budget item in this section is the interest expenses on our debt. About $220 billion, or 6%, was spent to attract parties to loan money to the government because our expenditures and tax revenues do not match up. (The accumulated national debt stood at about $11 trillion at the end of FY2012.)

The last "fifth" is a hodge podge of expenditures that includes funds for federal retirees, veterans, transportation infrastructure, food and drug protection, scientific and medical research, and humanitarian efforts around the world.

To summarize, our federal tax dollar is paying for:

21% : Medicare, Medicaid, and CHIP

21% : Medicare, Medicaid, and CHIP

22% : Social Security

19% : National Defense

12% : Safety net programs (e.g. SSI, food stamps, foster and adoptive care)

 7% : veterans and federal employee retires

 6% : interest on the debt

 2% : education

 3% : transportation

 2% : scientific and medical research

 5% : all other

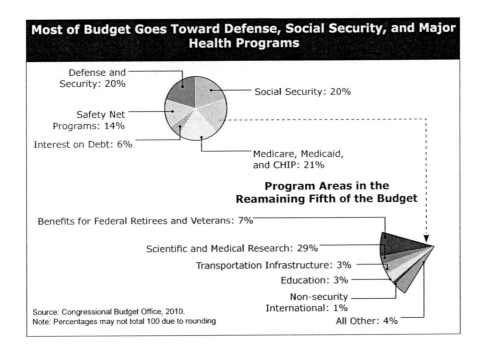

Most of Budget Goes Toward Defense, Social Security, and Major Health Programs

Defense and Security: 20%

Social Security: 20%

Safety Net Programs: 14%

Interest on Debt: 6%

Medicare, Medicaid, and CHIP: 21%

Program Areas in the Reamaining Fifth of the Budget

Benefits for Federal Retirees and Veterans: 7%

Scientific and Medical Research: 29%

Transportation Infrastructure: 3%

Education: 3%

Non-security International: 1%

All Other: 4%

Source: Congressional Budget Office, 2010.
Note: Percentages may not total 100 due to rounding

The Center on Budget and Policy Priorities provides the commonly used "pie chart" to describe the federal government's FY2012 budget thusly:

That's the picture for the central government. What about the budgets of the 50 states?

State:

As the matrix indicated, the #1 responsibility of state government is education. There is a significant difference in the sums that states will spend on the service, but it is clear that education is a state's top priority. According to the Center on Budget and Policy Priorities, state governments average 25% of their budgets on K-12 education, and spend another 14% on higher education (Center on Budget and Policy Priorities, 2012). State governments join the feds in paying for the Medicaid program, and significant sums are spent on transportation and corrections.

To summarize, our state tax dollar is paying for

25% : K-12 education

15% : Medicaid and other health care related programs

14% : Higher education (universities, community colleges, vocational education)

5% : Roads, bridges, public transit systems

5% : Prison systems and juvenile justice programs

1% : General welfare cash assistance

35% : Miscellaneous services and programs include state police, parks, economic development, environmental programs, and state employee retiree benefits

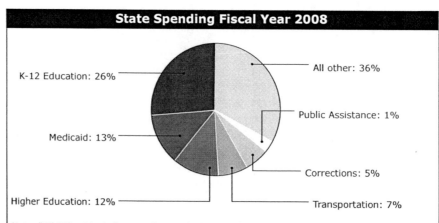

State Spending Fiscal Year 2008

K-12 Education: 26%

All other: 36%

Public Assistance: 1%

Medicaid: 13%

Corrections: 5%

Higher Education: 12%

Transportation: 7%

Note: "All Other" includes care for residents with disabilities, pensions, and health benefits foru public employees, enconomic development, environmental projects, state police, parks and recreation, and general aid to local governments. Totals may not sum due to rounding

Source: NASBO State Expendituer Report FY 2008, December 2009.

While variations occur among the states, the Center on Budget and Policy Priorities estimates the following percentages for the state budgets in FY2012

Local:

Local governments consist of county, city, municipal, village, and unincorporated regions, and services will vary according to the size of the jurisdiction. But, there is no question that the main service of local government is public safety, i.e. police protection and, in most cases, fire protection and emergency medical service. But, most local districts also provide public utilities (water, sewer, and trash removal), and road maintenance and repair is a third common provision. In larger local jurisdictions, services for public transportation, parks and recreation, and economic development are rendered.

Taxes

People often complain that their taxes are too high, and while it is rather axiomatic that the current U.S. tax code is unwieldy and needs major reform, it is really a rather silly statement to utter. Of course, no one wishes to pay any more tax than is necessary (and America enjoys one of the lowest tax burdens around the world, by the way), so the true heart of the complaint is that the critic probably believes that the scope of government is too big and/or the government is spending funds on services that are not a priority to him.

The debate about the size of government and its priorities is a discussion always worth having, but once it has been determined what services governments are to render, taxes are just a way to raise the revenue that is needed to provide them.

Governments actually can raise funds from a variety of strategies. First, it can charge a fee just like a private sector business might charge to its customer. Local governments charge fees for marriage licenses, state governments can charge fees for drivers' licenses and license plates, and the federal government charges entrance fees into its national parks.

And, governments can use what are called excise taxes, i.e. taxes that target specific products such as cigarettes, gasoline, or yachts. Smokers often develop health care issues that are expensive to address, expenses that are often beyond their health insurance, so the cigarette tax acquires funds ahead of the time that will likely be needed to provide health care to the person suffering from emphysema. People who travel in vehicles put wear and tear on those roads, necessitating repair at some point, so the government levies a tax on the users of roads, i.e. parties who buy gasoline, to obtain the funds ahead of time to pay for the eventual repairs. And, yachts (and expensive cars and jewelry) are taxed simply because they can only be purchased by the wealthy – who can afford to pay a luxury tax.

But, while governments can raise funds in a variety of ways, its main strategies are taxing income, sales, and property.

Income taxes:

Income Tax: is a tax levied on wages and corporate profits.

We are all familiar with April 15th "tax day." Actually, April 15th is really nothing more than the deadline for reconciliation, balancing the amount of tax that a taxpayer owes and the amount of tax that has already been paid. The form we all fill out is just the process of determining one's taxable income, and then using the relevant strategy for calculating the tax. After then comparing how much tax may have already been paid to how much is owed, the taxpayer may owe some more, or perhaps he/she overpaid, i.e. is entitled to a refund. But, while the theory is simple, the headaches come from all the gymnastics in determining one's taxable income (which is not the same as one's annual salary(ies) because of exemptions and deduction possibilities, and then "calculating" the tax owed.

Excise Tax: are levies on targeted items such as cigarettes and gasoline.

Individual income taxes make up the largest source of revenue for the federal government, followed by the payroll tax on wages for the Social Security program, followed by the corporate income tax, followed by the payroll tax on wages for the Medicare program, followed by the business tax on employee wages for the Unemployment Insurance program, followed by excise taxes.

(To supplement taxes, the federal government gets revenue from selling items and services, and borrows money by selling bonds and other federal securities.)

Sales taxes:

Sales Tax: is a levy on purchases made by customers.

A sales tax is a tax on consumption; the tax is paid on the value of the consumption transaction. States can also gain revenue from income taxes, fees, business taxes, and even lotteries, but the principal source is the sales tax. The sales tax is rather simple and straightforward, difficult to avoid, and is easy to collect.

Historically, states garner about 50% of their needed revenue from this single source.

VAT tax:

The U.S. has begun debating the worthiness of another version of a sales tax called VAT: Value Added Tax. It is essentially a national sales tax, although the tax is paid all along the production and distribution process. It is only paid on the value *added* by various parties in the production-distribution process. For instance, a VAT tax is levied when raw materials are sold to a manufacturer, when the manufacturer sells the produced good to a wholesaler, when the wholesaler sells the item to a retailer, and when the retailer sells the item to the consumer. But, businesses get tax credits for VAT taxes paid at the previous stage, so only new value added by the business is taxed.

Property Tax: is a levy on the value of real estate.

Property taxes:

A property tax levies a tax on the value of real estate. A local authority appraises the estimated value of the property, and a rate is assessed according to the local council. Local governments can charge fees and business taxes, and a few cities charge a local income tax. But, the property tax remains the major source of funds for local services.

Proportional: means all payers have the same burden.

PROPORTIONAL, REGRESSIVE, and PROGRESSIVE TAXES

What makes a good tax system? Adam Smith, the founder of capitalism, contended that a good tax system was one that was efficient to collect, i.e. the costs of collection were low, the timing and amount of tax were knowable to the taxpayer, the timing of tax payment was reasonably convenient, and taxes levied should be based upon the taxpayer's ability to pay. Over the years, economists have added additional features, including a sense of fairness. While few people enjoy paying taxes, a good system is one in which taxpayers believe they are being taxed equitably.

But, just what does "equitably" mean? If you ask 10 people, you are liable to get 11 answers regarding just what constitutes fair tax treatment. To some, it means levying everyone the same amount, i.e. everyone pays the same tax of, say $100. To others, it means levying the same percentage on everyone, i.e. everyone pays the same, say 5%, on their income, their retail purchase, their property, or whatever the base of the tax is. But, to still others, fairness means that people of different means should pay at different rates. So, we now need a brief discussion of the different kinds of *tax burdens.*

Proportional:

Proportional taxes are perhaps the easiest to grasp since everyone is treated "the same." When people cite examples of a proportional tax, they often cite a state's income tax or a state's sales tax. In either tax, each taxpayer pays at the same rate as every other taxpayer. For example, if the state's income tax rate is 4%, that rate applies to all citizens with taxable income. Whether one's income is $25,000, $50,000, or $75,000, each earner faces the same rate, i.e. 4%.

Similarly, if the state's sales tax is 6%, every customer faces the same tax rate every time he or she makes a purchase. The amount of consumption (the purchase) may be low or high, but the same 6% applies to everyone alike.

On the surface, this sameness observation is quite correct. When there is but one tax rate, all taxpayers face it. But, the *burden* of the tax is not necessarily the same. The burden of a tax depends upon one's ability to pay the tax, based on their income. So, let's revisit our examples above.

If the income tax rate is 4%, will the $25,000 income earner pay the same amount of tax as the $50,000 earner? No. Because his income is twice as much, the $50,000 wage earner will pay twice as much tax as the $25,000 wage earner. But, while the actual tax sums will be different, the burden of the tax sum will be identical, i.e. each will pay 4% of his income. The $50,000 wage earner will pay $2,000 in income taxes (as opposed to the $1,000 that the $25,000 earner will pay), but because he has twice as much income, he can afford the higher tax payment. Each person will have the same burden on his income. So, a state income tax is a good example of a proportional tax: **the burden of the tax is the same at all income levels.**

But, recall a sales tax is a tax on consumption, not on income. Hence, a sales tax is not based upon one's ability to pay. It is true that one's general level of consumption can be somewhat consistent with one's income level; i.e., the $50,000 income earner won't face the sales tax sum on the purchase of an expensive car because he won't be buying the expensive car in the first place, and such an argument about the fairness of a sales tax is acceptable when thinking about "luxury" purchases or even "high quality" purchases when lower priced options are available to the low(er) income families. But, some consumption is pretty basic to all, and the fairness feature of the sales tax (or any *ad valorem* tax) can be questioned.

Regressive:

Regressive: means the tax burden is higher on lower income payers.

Unlike a proportional tax whose burden is the same, i.e. proportional to all payers of the tax, a regressive tax is one in which the burdens are not equal. Indeed, the definition of a **regressive tax is a tax whose burden is higher in lower incomes.**

Consider our sales tax again. While it is true, American free enterprise typically offers product and service options at different price levels so that consumers can often find the product or service they need at a price they can afford, that isn't as feasible with products that are considered necessities. Food is probably the most basic purchase there is, but all sales tax schemes exempt all or most food items (though items like tooth paste and tooth brushes are often not exempt), so the unfairness of differing burdens is minimized. But, if we take another necessity purchase such as underwear, socks, or belts, there isn't that much difference in the price paid by the wealthy consumer and the price a low income consumer must pay. Hence, on a purchase of a few packages of undershirts, the sales tax will be essentially the same amount for most all taxpayers, but the burden of that tax will be higher for the low income person to handle. Multiply such a transaction times many other necessity purchases in a year, and the burden can become real.

Or, consider the property tax. A tax is levied on the value of a house or a piece of land, regardless of the income the property owner has. At one time in our history, the property tax was used because only the wealthy could afford to own a home. It was essentially a tax on the rich. But, over the centuries, and especially since WWII when home ownership was promoted as the centerpiece of the American dream for all Americans, millions now are homeowners. However, the tax is on the value of the property, not on the income of the home owner, so a property tax on a $150,000 home is much harder for a $40,000 wage earner than for one making $70,000. To be sure, a lower or even middle income earner should not be buying a "high priced" house, but consider that plight of millions of U.S. seniors who paid off the mortgage while still working, but who are now retired and living off Social Security and whatever private retirement benefits they may have.

Progressive:

The federal income tax is the best example of a progressive tax scheme. In a proportional tax scheme (e.g. a state income tax), the tax burden is the same even though the tax amounts are different. That sameness of burden occurred because everyone paid at the same tax rate. But, not only do Americans pay different sums of federal income tax because incomes are different, Americans will pay different tax amounts because the federal income tax system uses different tax rates depending upon one's level of income. Before the 1980's, the U.S. tax code included 7 different rates (including one as high as 90% back in the 1950's), but President Reagan spent much of his second term in the mid-1980's pushing for tax reforms, including a reduction of the tax rates to only three. (Rates and income brackets can be adjusted by the Congress, but roughly speaking, we have a rate of about 15% for taxable incomes between the minimum and $30,000, a rate of about 25% for incomes between $30,000 and $80,000, and a rate of about 35% for incomes above $80,000) (Should you mention that the wealthy rarely pay this percentage because they have so many loopholes to avoid taxes?)

Progressive: means the tax burden is higher on the higher income payers

But, because there are (3) different tax rates, that means the taxpayer making $100,000 will not only pay more taxes than someone earning $50,000 because he has more income, he will pay more taxes because he faces a higher tax rate. Hence, **a progressive tax is a tax whose burden is higher on higher incomes.**

So, is the American tax system fair? Again, that depends on one's definition of "equitable."

DO BUDGET DEFICITS MATTER?

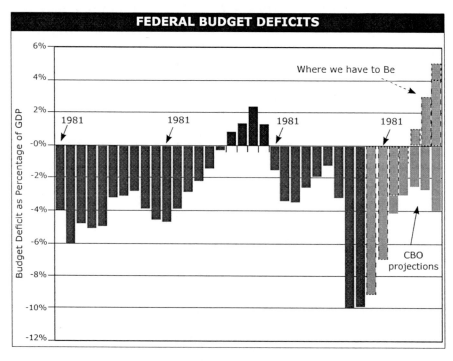

FEDERAL BUDGET DEFICITS

Budget Deficit: *means expenses are greater than revenue.*

A deficit means that expenses exceed revenue; businesses experience losses all the time. But when a business has a loss, it must find a solution. If the business has sufficient savings, the loss is covered by transferring the needed sum from savings. Or, if the business has no savings, it will need to seek a loan from a bank, or, if a corporation, sell bonds or stock to private investors. And, throughout the year, monitoring the situation could warn business leaders that to avoid the loss, it might need to cut expenses and/or raise its prices.

If we apply the same scenario to a family, the options are similar. The family needs more income (someone gets a second job or a higher paying first job), or some expenses are reduced or eliminated altogether. Or, the solution many Americans have been fond of using for the past decade or so, is to "finance" the extra expenses via charge cards, which means that the family is spending their *future* income before they even earn it. This is how many families, though certainly not all, got into trouble in the Great Recession of 2008.

How does this apply to the nation's federal budget? Annual deficits mean that we have spent more dollars on programs and services than we have received in taxes and fees. And, unless and until we either raise more revenue and/or cut or eliminate programs and services, the government borrows money from private investors.

Economists generally agree that a country's government pretty much needs to incur deficits when facing mitigating circumstances such as war or a widespread financial crisis. Usually it is more important to spend funds to address/resolve the circumstances than it is balance the budget; borrowing is necessary.

But, routine borrowing means that the government hasn't satisfactorily addressed the need to raise more revenue and/or cut expenses (usually because of differences between the political parties over the perceived priorities of the country). And, there are a couple of problems associated with borrowing that is persistent and growing. First, there are only so many private investors, and it isn't healthy for the government to compete with businesses for the available savings of the country. The more the government successfully borrows, the fewer investor dollars for private enterprises to acquire. (That of course assumes that the economy is robust and businesses wish to borrow. If the economy is not robust, any "crowding out" by government is modest.) Second, borrowers can lose confidence in the government and its ability to repay its loans, which will cause one of two bad results: 1) investors will only loan funds to the government at higher interest rates, which of course worsens the U.S. debt, and 2) the investors decide not to loan money any longer to the U.S. government. Should that day ever occur, the U.S., like a family, would have no recourse but to raise taxes and/or slash programs and services.

Deficits are not always avoidable, but America's indebtedness needs to be significantly reduced. Americans need to get serious about developing better agreements on what the scope of government services should be, and then pretty much staying within those annual budgets. (It should be pointed out that America's deficit has been reduced under Obama, and that the current recalcitrant Congress makes it impossible to come to any economic agreements)

WHAT IS SEQUESTRATION?

In its essence, economics is about making choices; and making choices is reflected in how values and priorities are satisfied. Pursuing program and service priorities is where economics and politics intersect, and a major reason for America's growing budget deficits is our country's inability to develop sufficient political compromises. Given the consistently narrow margins that presidential winners have received since the 1990's, it is becoming rather evident that America is struggling to reach a consensus regarding our economic priorities and how to achieve them. Instead of compromises facilitated by moderates in our political parties, political representatives have become more and more "extreme" in their respective views with, each side asserting that it is saving America's future from the other. Americans seem to be pretty well evenly divided philosophically. We cannot seem to form a consensus on economic values and priorities, and the political "gridlock", has made finding common ground and negotiating solutions on budget issues all but impossible.

Hence, we seem to be stuck in a pattern of spending more on programs and services than we have revenue to support. One party believes that the "haves" should be paying more in taxes, and both parties agree that long term debt is bad and annual government spending should be reduced, but they vehemently disagree about which programs and services should be cut, and by how much. And, add debates about military interventions into the discussion, and any budget "negotiations" become quagmired quickly.

Yet, while all politicians acknowledge that the current pattern (ongoing deficits) is "unsustainable," middle ground seems to elude them. So, to motivate itself to enter into those tough negotiations, Congress (the Gramm-Rudman-Hollings Act in 1985, later amended in 1990 by PAYGO bill), passed legislation to trigger what was thought to be a devastating strategy of automatic and draconian cuts in federal government spending if politicians failed to hammer out something more sensible. Somewhat like "playing chicken", if lawmakers failed to take responsible action, both sides would lose. Program/service reductions would be activated automatically due to Congress' inaction, and cuts would have nothing to do with how "essential" a program or service might be. As analysts were fond of saying, the spending cuts would be done with an axe instead of a scalpel. Thus, this insensitive strategy was to prevent foot-dragging and motivate warring political factions to work something out.

The PAYGO law expired in 2002, but the sequestration idea was resurrected and embedded in the budget resolution of 2011. It was scheduled to kick in, if needed, on January 1 of 2013. Frustratingly, it was needed, though it was delayed until March, 2013.

So, what have been the consequences of the sequestration implementation? For starters, some major government programs are exempt, most notably Social Security, Medicaid, federal worker pensions, and veterans' benefits. Medicare spending will be reduced by a static 2% a year (unless Congress acts to amend this rate), and a variety of defense and non-defense programs and services were cut by percentages ranging from 5% to 10%, depending on the program/service. So, thousands of government employees will be "furloughed", perhaps eventually laid off. There will be fewer health inspections, less monitoring of alleged pollution, reduced training for troops, slower criminal prosecutions, fewer small business loans, and so on. Additionally, hundreds of programs, mostly for America's low income or otherwise disadvantaged citizens, will render less service to fewer recipients. Furloughed/laid off workers will spend less in the towns where they reside, but because the deficit and debt will be lower, interest payments will decrease.

A Gallup Poll taken in July of 2013 indicated that 15% of Americans thought the sequestration cutting of government programs was "good", 30% thought it was "bad", and 55% "don't know enough to say" (Jones, 2013).

Again, America is in the midst of "sorting out" its values and cultural priorities, and it is unclear just what the majority of Americans want the role of government to be. Stay tuned.

CHAPTER SUMMARY

Fiscal policy and monetary policy are the two general strategies of governmental intervention to promote our economy's three foundational economic goals. Monetary policy (last chapter) concerns the government's attempt to monitor and control the economy's money supply, and fiscal policy regards the government's right to levy taxes to then spend on programs and services. Government spending equals about 25% of our country's GDP.

All levels of government provide services and programs, and public safety is a common theme. The federal government's major expenditures are Social Security, Medicare, (Medicaid?) and national defense. State governments spend taxes on education, welfare, and state police/corrections. Local governments spend funds on police and fire protection, city utilities, and streets and gutters.

The size of government, as well as the services and programs it provides, is one controversy; how those government services are paid for is another public policy debate. Technically, the government can levy a tax on anything it politically approves, but modern America tends to raise most of its tax revenues from three bases: 1) income, 2) sales, and 3) property. The federal government, most state governments, and many city governments use income taxes as a major source of revenue; most states use a sales tax to raise funds, and all local governments reply heavily on property taxes to fund their services. Excise taxes are also rather common, e.g., gasoline, cigarettes, et al. (You may recall from your history books that the British government levied a tax on tea that turned out to be quite "unpopular" with certain Boston residents.)

While no one enjoys paying taxes, taxpayers would at least the like the tax to be levied fairly; but, "fairly" may not mean the same thing to everyone. A proportional tax, such as most state income taxes, is a tax in which the burden of the tax is the same for all taxpayers. A progressive tax, such as the federal income tax, is a tax in which the burden is higher on higher income taxpayers. And, a regressive tax, such a sales tax or a property tax, is a tax in which the burden of the tax is higher on lower income taxpayers. What is fair? What is a fair tax? Everyone pays the same tax sum? Everyone pays the same burden? Those with more ability to pay should shoulder a higher burden? Tax rates become yet another public policy controversy.

Lastly, governments often have more demands for programs and services that they have funds to pay for them, especially when the economy is declining. Unless government makes the necessary budget cuts in programs and services to equal its decreasing tax revenues, budget deficits will occur. And, the deficit means that more money must be raised, and governments raise the needed extra funds by borrowing, i.e. selling bonds (IOU's). Bonds must be repaid, with interest, so, while the maintenance of the government programs and services may be deemed very important, citizens need to know that borrowing means that the country is spending future revenue, and interest is a cost that future revenue will also need to repay.

Furthermore, there are only so many parties with an ability and/ or interest to loan funds to parties looking to borrow, so government borrowing can sometimes "crowd out" some of the private sector's ability to acquire borrowed funds for business needs since loaners will loan to the U.S. government (a much lower risk than ABC Corporation) rather than private businesses unless private businesses are willing to offer higher interest rates. Forcing private sector corporations to compete with governments to borrow funds only raises rates or precludes the business borrowing altogether. Neither development helps an economy recover.

▶▶| *Chapter 11 Review*

Key concepts:

1. Fiscal policy regards the government's right to tax and spend.

2. Governments should provide "public good" services and products: items that are jointly used and determination of exclusive consumption is not possible. For example, all Americans derive a national security benefit from our armed services, but it is not possible to identify which soldier, tank, or plane is defending which taxpayer.

3. The federal government's major services are Social Security, Medicare, and national defense, and it relies mostly in income taxes.

4. State governments focus primarily on education, welfare, and state police/ corrections, and states mostly rely on sales taxes.

5. Local governments rely mostly on property taxes to provide police and fire protection, city utilities, and streets and gutters.

6. Tax philosophies are: 1) progressive (tax burden is higher on higher income taxpayers), 2) proportional (tax burdens are equal on all taxpayers, or 3) regressive (tax burden is higher on lower income taxpayers).

7. Budget deficits occur when revenues do not match needed/desired spending, and the federal government borrows extra money by selling bonds to wealthy parties. But, borrowing creates interest expenses that must be paid from future revenue, and government borrowing can create problems for private sector businesses who may also wish to borrow funds.

Key terms:

fiscal policy, income tax, excise tax, sales tax, VAT, property tax, progressive tax, proportional tax, regressive tax, budget deficit

CHAPTER

12

UNEMPLOYMENT & INFLATION: CAUSES AND SOLUTIONS

From prior chapters we know that our free market economy seeks to achieve three foundational economic goals – economic growth, "full" employment, and price stability – and when we fail to accomplish them, we risk their subsequent economic ailments, namely unemployment and inflation. This chapter is devoted to a better understanding of their causes and possible solutions.

EMPLOYMENT BASICS

The U.S. Labor Force:

We make an effort to take a head count (a census) in our country every ten years, and the latest occurred in 2010, though the results won't be "known" until 2011 or even 2012. We say "known" because the census is never completely accurate, but we can make reasonable estimates, including the anticipated size of the population. A growing population is usually a positive development, though historical economists such as Thomas Malthus contended that too much population could outstrip the nation's ability to feed people and famine and war could result. But, so far, U.S. ingenuity and technological advancement has prevented such a dire prediction, but paying attention to one's population is important.

Labor Force: regards persons in the population able to work.

While the total population of the United States is a bit above 300 million people, not all are part of the labor force. Children under the age of 16 and retired senior citizens are not counted, nor are people who are institutionalized (e.g. prisons or mental facilities). And, military personnel who are serving overseas are also not included. So, our definition of the labor force is all non-institutionalized persons who are working or looking for work less those who are under age or armed service personnel outside the country.

So, how many people is that? How many Americans are typically in the labor force? At the beginning of the 21st century, there were roughly 140 million persons in our labor force, and that number has increased to approximately 155 million workers in 2010, but as the chart below indicates, the participation rate of the civilian labor force has risen from 58.5% after WWII and is now in the 65-67.5 % range:

The increase is a double edged sword. On the one hand, general growth in economic activity (production) cannot be accomplished with a sufficient number of workers. Technological innovations can offset the need for some of the needed growth, but machines cannot handle all production tasks. At least, not yet. So, if a country's GDP and standard of living are to expand, a growing number of workers is likely needed to facilitate the expansion.

On the other hand, if the increases in the labor force are greater than the increases in the economy's production activities, i.e. the economy does not expand fast enough to keep up with the growing numbers on the labor force, the country winds up with an excess supply of labor. What happens to prices when supply is greater than demand? When there are more workers willing to supply their labor than there is a demand for workers by businesses, wages are affected. And, stagnant or low wages can cause even more people to enter the labor force (or remain in the labor force longer) which cause other (mostly social) problems.

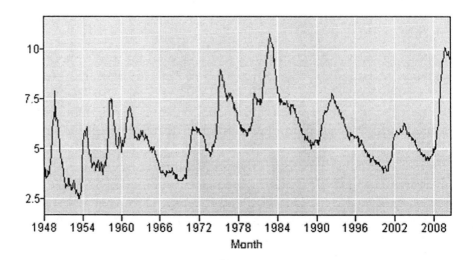

Calculating Unemployment:

Actually, the word 'calculating' is probably misleading; unemployment numbers and, therefore, unemployment rates are estimated. It was noted earlier that the total labor force is defined as those who are working or seeking work, so we define the unemployed as those who are not working, but are actively seeking work. Once we have estimates of the (civilian) labor force and the unemployed, the unemployment rate is merely a ratio, i.e. the number of unemployed divided by the number in the labor force. Hence, the key to "calculating" the unemployment rate is the estimate of the number of unemployed people.

Unemployment: regards people in the labor force who are not working, but are looking for work

Many students, or Americans, in general, no doubt think the number of unemployed people should be easy to determine; just add up the claims being filed in state and federal unemployment benefits programs.

Perhaps, but such a count would be immediately inaccurate for at least a couple of reasons. First, many workers are eligible for unemployment benefits, but don't file for them. Second, many workers run out of unemployment benefits, but are still seeking employment. So, such a strategy won't really identify the scope of the issue. And, since literally contacting every household every month to count the unemployed is impractical (and costly), the government uses a different approach.

The federal government conducts a monthly Current Population Survey (CPS) to estimate the extent of unemployment. This survey, while revised and revised, has been undertaken every month since 1940, and some 60,000 households are sampled, which means that over 100,000 people are contacted on a monthly basis. It is sufficient to conclude here that measures are taken to ensure new households are constantly being contacted, i.e. the same parties are not being repeatedly sampled, and such a survey sample far exceeds the polling we routinely use for political elections.

In 2010, the U.S. was still in one of the worst financial periods in its existence, second only to the Great Depression (when unemployment was nearly 25%), and unemployment as of this writing exceeds 9%, but the graph below provides a historical view:

We need to make one last observation regarding the unemployment rate. Recall that the unemployment rate is based upon the number of estimated unemployed people, but the definition of unemployed people regards workers who are out of work, but are still looking for work. First, people who are employed part-time, but would prefer full-time work (called the under-employed), are not considered unemployed. Second, workers who are out of work, but who have given up the search (called discouraged workers), are also not technically considered unemployed. Hence, our final observation on the subject is that the true percentage of unemployed persons in the country is always higher than the official, stated measure.

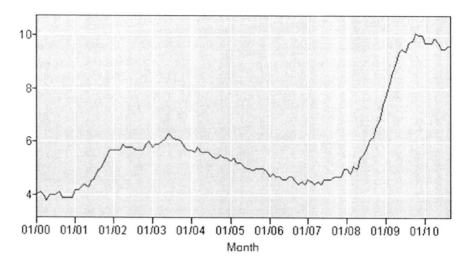

(For instance, in 2010, while the official unemployment rate hovers between 9.5% and 10%, economists estimate the figure to be as high as 17%.)

Labor Force Characteristics and Trends

Over the last several decades, the U.S. population has increased, and so have both the labor force and the participation rate. But, over the next few decades, the U.S. labor force is expected to grow only modestly (at rates of less than 1% a year), so as Baby Boomers retire, it is unclear whether the U.S. will have enough workers to facilitate future growth in the economy's GDP. And, the composition of the American labor force is changing rather significantly. Let's look at the demographics and project.

Gender:

Fifty years ago, 85% of men were in the U.S. labor force, while only 40% of women held a job outside the home. Men made up 60% of the labor force, and women 40%. But, with the advent of the social revolution of the 1960's and/or suppressed wages, in general, more and more women entered the labor force in the last 35 years, so that the participation rate of women has increased to 60%, i.e. the majority of women work outside the home, and now 70% of men work. It is estimated that presently 52% of the labor force is male and 48% is female.

That participation rate trend is expected to continue, i.e. the percentage increase of women in the labor force will be greater than the percentage increase of men. It won't be long when the labor force will be 50-50. That has major implications for employers or society at large since flexible work schedules and/or child care resources will be

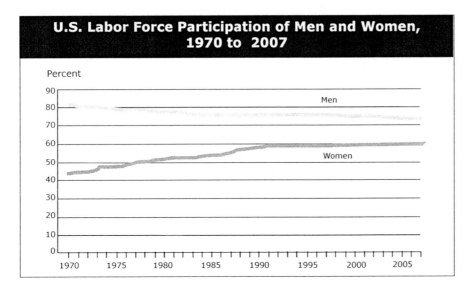

essential to maintain needed women in the workforce. So, it is unclear whether female participation rates in the labor force have peaked or will rise, especially if child care accommodations will be forthcoming.

Age:

The chart below rather clearly indicates that the general age of the U.S. workforce is rising; see below:

While Baby Boomers are expected to retire – eventually – recent economic crises have forestalled that day for millions of older workers.

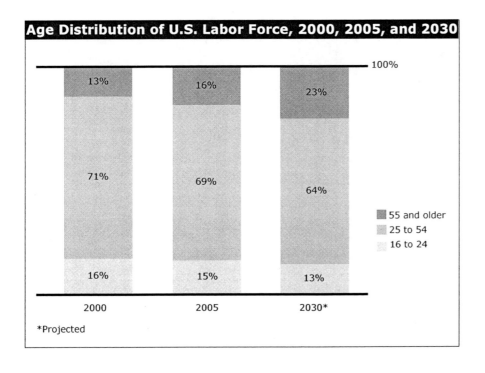

Retirement has all but risen from 65 to 70, and, sadly, the decline in the percentage of the labor force at the younger ages is at least partially attributable to insufficient education for many, especially minority males.

Race and Ethnicity:

It is clear that the dominance of the U.S. labor force by whites is coming to an end, probably around the middle of this century. Hispanics have overtaken Blacks as the largest minority race, and the fastest growth rates in labor participation will occur in the Asian and Hispanic races. These trends are noted by the chart and pie graph below:

Racial Make-Up of U.S. Labor Force (in thousands)

Ethnicity	1980	1990	2000	2010 (Projection)
White	87,454 (81.8%)	96,727	102,206	107,096 (67.9%)
Black	10,865 (10.2%)	13,740	16,603	20,041 (12.7%)
Hispanic	6,146 (5.7%)	10,720	15,368	20,947 (13.3%)
Asian/Other	2,476 (2.3%)	4,653	6,687	9,636 (6.1%)
Total	106,940	125,840	140,863	157,721

Source: Fullerton and Toossi, Monthly Labor Review, 2001

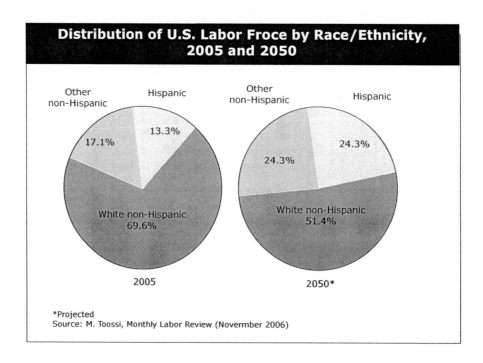

Distribution of U.S. Labor Froce by Race/Ethnicity, 2005 and 2050

Other non-Hispanic Hispanic

13.3%

17.1%

White non-Hispanic
69.6%

2005

Other non-Hispanic Hispanic

24.3%

24.3%

White non-Hispanic
51.4%

2050*

*Projected
Source: M. Toossi, Monthly Labor Review (Novermber 2006)

CAUSES of UNEMPLOYMENT:

Recessions often follow the end of wars, and 1946 was no exception. WWII lasted 4 years, and by the time the GI's came home from Europe and/or the Pacific, the U.S. labor force had made adjustments. Hence, upon their return, there was an excess supply of labor, and an economy that had been busy making planes and bullets and uniforms needed to be re-tooled. But, that would take time to sort out, and in the meantime, ex-soldiers were out of work. So, Congress passed the Full Employment Act of 1946, vowing to make employment a high priority. While employment is of course still one of our "Top 3" economic goals, 100% employment is not realistic. Given our modern, mobile society, "full" employment has come to mean about 96% employment.

Hence, policy makers don't get too excited until unemployment starts to move from 4% towards 5% or higher.

Frictional:

Frictional unemployment is voluntary unemployment, and policy makers don't worry too much about such workers. Someone who has been an insurance salesman for 20 years in New England wakes up one morning and decides he doesn't want to endure one more winter of cold and snow, so he packs up his family and relocates to warmer climates. He has no job lined up; he just moves and lives off his savings until he finds employment in the south. Our society is highly mobile, and workers resign all the time to "start over" somewhere else. They are unemployed, but they are usually successful in acquiring a new opportunity relatively quickly.

Frictional Unemployment: regards people who are voluntarily unemployed.

Seasonal:

Nearly every business and industry has a peak time and a slow period, and often firms will need to add temporary employees during the busy season and/or lay off employees during the slack season. For example, landscaping can only be performed in the spring, summer, and fall months in the northern states, so, unless such businesses can shift into snow plowing services for the winter period, some landscaping workers will not be needed during the winter.

Cyclical:

Our economy expands and then contracts in cycles. The nature of market forces are such that economic growth is not sustainable "forever"; the economy expands and expands and expands, but then aggregate demand slackens, and businesses have too many resources for the slowed economy. Hence, layoffs occur. If business managers and CEO's could forecast perfectly, excess resources, including labor, wouldn't be compiled in the first place, but hindsight, not vision, is 20-20. Recessions do occur while the economy "takes a breath", and some workers lose their positions.

Usually, it is the least productive workers that are laid off, i.e. the employees with the lowest skills and/or least amount of education and experience, but some employers use recessions as an opportunity to shed expensive workers, i.e. those with high salaries. Employers may also "replace" laid off workers with some sort of technological addition that can absorb the subsequent resurgence in economic growth without re-hiring former workers.

Cyclically unemployed workers usually find employment with the former employer, and often in the same position as before. But, sometimes, workers may find similar employment as before, but with a new employer. And, sometimes the worker may need to change career paths and pursue a different position with a different employer in a different industry.

Structural:

Structural Unemployment: regards workers whose skill and/or knowledge are no longer valued by the economy.

Structural unemployment is, in this author's opinion, the more worrisome category of unemployment because this situation is caused by progress and innovation. Structural unemployment occurs when employees have skills and knowledge that are no longer valued by the economic. Hence, these are not workers with no skill or no education; they simply now have an outmoded skill or yesterday's wisdom.

For a simplistic example, at the turn of the 20th century, there must have been many buggy whip manufacturers. People traveled by buggy and carriage, so every driver needed such a product to get a horse's attention. I would imagine that, among the many buggy whip makers, there was the low price option, the high quality option, and various alternatives of price and quality in between. Employees were no doubt dedicated craftsmen who took pride in their work. But, along came an entrepreneur by the name of Henry Ford who invented the Model-T Ford automobile, and the rest is history. Those hard-working and talented craftsmen had a skill the economy no longer valued, and they were soon quite unemployed. They did nothing wrong, unless you fault a worker for failing to see the future. They were simply victims of technological advancement and product innovation. But, such unemployment should be a reminder to each one of us to keep an eye on competitive, technological, legal, political, and even demographic changes to appreciate their potential impact on one's job security.

There is only one solution to such a development: acquire a skill and/or knowledge that the economy does value. Millions of American employees go back to school for that very reason, and millions more maintain/ update/expand their skills to be in a better position to accommodate such invention/innovation changes in our economy's growth.

Minimum Wage:

Minimum Wage is the government's controversial attempt to assist low income earners. The idea is to provide a floor below which (most) workers cannot be paid, i.e. most everyone is guaranteed a minimum. (Some workers are not covered by minimum wage law.) The original minimum wage was 25 cents set in 1938 by the Fair Labor Standards Act. The federal legislation has been amended many times over the years, with the most recent increases in 1996-97 (from $4.25 to $5.15 an hour), 2007 (from $5.15 to $5.85 an hour), 2008 (from $5.85 to $6.55 an hour), and then the latest increase occurred in 2009 to $7.25 per hour. Some states also have minimum wage laws, and an eligible employee is entitled to the higher of the two rates.

Two observations are worth our attention. First, the vast majority of employees are paid sums above the minimum wage, so relatively few are directly affected. According to the Bureau of Labor Statistics, 3.6 million workers were paid at the minimum wage level (in 2012), which of course is a great many families, but these represent 4.7% of the labor force. The vast majority are employed in the leisure and hospitality industries (fast food, overnight lodging, and tourism). Women, part-time workers, and minorities are the most impacted. And, about a third of the minimum wage employees are teenagers. (Think fast food restaurants.)

Second, critics contend that the minimum wage strategy is counter-productive. By requiring that wages be increased, a business now faces increased expenses, and one of three consequences will occur: 1) the firm will accept lower profits than would otherwise be the case, 2) the firm will raise its prices to maintain its desired profits, or 3) the firm will lay off employees to keep the total payroll expenses at the needed level when the law took effect. For most firms, that's a no brainer; they lay off employees. The remaining employees are better paid, but now there are fewer of them, so they must somehow become more efficient to pick up the work formerly handled by the terminated workers. And, who are the most likely employees to be laid off? The very ones that the minimum wage was supposed to help, i.e. the employees with the lowest skills/education.

One last thought. The minimum wage is not the same thing as a livable wage. Those who advocate for the minimum wage complain that it should be raised (and raised and raised) because one cannot live on such a low rate.

Minimum Wage: regards a price floor for wages.

Yes, that's probably true. But, the minimum wage was never intended to be a livable wage. Inflation as well as the growing disparity in wage levels (discussed in a later chapter) have made it more difficult for minimum wage earners to make ends meet, but whether the minimum wage should be enough to raise a family on is a matter of serious political dispute. It is true that attempts to increase the minimum wage, usually by one of the major political parties, are often blocked by the other major political party due to significant philosophical differences. Recent Gallop polls (March, 2013, and November, 2013) due indicate that 71% - 76%, respectively, but it is unclear whether polled Americans fully understand the economic implications. If employers are faced with rising costs due to required wage increases, one of three results will likely occur: 1) profits will decrease, 2) some employees will be laid off to keep payroll expenses at the budgeted amount, or 3) prices will be raised to customers. The first option almost never occurs, so Americans who favor raising the minimum wage need to be willing to face the prospect of higher prices, and most polls don't include the questions that would help clarify/ confirm the American sentiment.

Some studies have shown that modest increases in the minimum wage can be more easily absorbed and employees need not be laid off, but there are also several studies that confirm an increase in personnel expenses leads to lost jobs. Hence, that's why the minimum wage public policy remains controversial.

SOLUTIONS to UNEMPLOYMENT:

Unemployment means, of course, that the supply of labor is greater than the demand for labor, i.e. there are more people wanting a job than there are businesses with job vacancies. And, while we know that there are 4 categories of unemployment, frictional is voluntary, seasonal is short-lived, and structural can occur in any industry at any time if some sort of innovation changes the skills that employees need. Hence, it is cyclical unemployment that occurs most often, and it is depicted in the graph below that shows the "shift" in the demand curve that created the unemployment problem.

There are two macro options: 1) if labor will be willing to work at lower wage levels, then the demand for labor could increase, thereby employing more people, or 2) create a "shift" back of demand for labor by stimulating more consumer purchasing.

Occasionally, workers are willing to accept pay cuts to prevent layoffs and/or laid off workers are willing to take a new job at a lower salary from another employer, but those developments are never widespread throughout the economy. Indeed, John Maynard Keynes' classical research indicated that wages were usually "sticky", that is, wages are rigid and unlikely to decline.

DEMAND "SHIFTS" INWARD

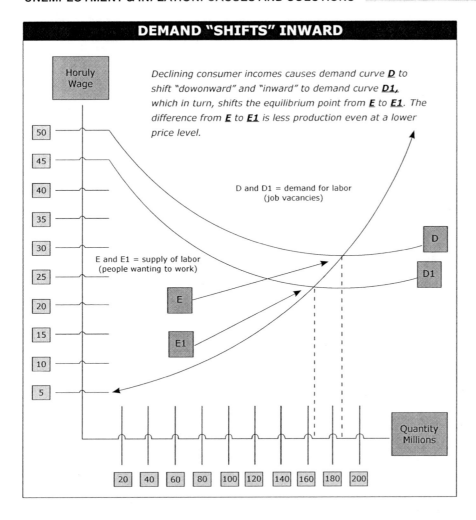

*Declining consumer incomes causes demand curve **D** to shift "dowonward" and "inward" to demand curve **D1**, which in turn, shifts the equilibrium point from **E** to **E1**. The difference from **E** to **E1** is less production even at a lower price level.*

D and D1 = demand for labor (job vacancies)

E and E1 = supply of labor (people wanting to work)

Most workers are willing to risk being a laid off worker versus maintaining the current wage, and most employers would prefer to keep solidly performing workers and lose the poor performing ones than keep all. Hence, pay cuts are rare; layoffs are common.

Hence, we are pragmatically left with the option that we must somehow boost aggregate consumer spending which should, in turn, ultimately increase the firm's need to hire more employees to keep up with the rising demand for goods and services. How can we do that? How can we stimulate consumer spending?

While our economic system has some "automatic stabilizers" to assist those who have lost their jobs continue to have funds to maintain some consumer spending (e.g. unemployment benefits), the matrix below pretty much covers the extra public policy strategies:

Fiscal Policy	Monetary Policy
The executive and legislative branches of the government can:	The Federal Reserve System can increase the money supply by:
• Lower taxes to give citizens more income to spend at their discretion	• Lowering the legal reserve requirement,

• Raise taxes and earmark the funds
  o hire firms to undertake valued projects (e.g., build a road
  o pursue education
	• Lowering the discount rate, and/ or

• Increase government spending for projects (like those above) without raising taxes	• Buying bonds

The school of thought that suggests that government intervention (to use tax or spending adjustments, i.e. fiscal policy) is commonly called the Keynesian view after British economist John Maynard Keynes who studied and wrote about unemployment in the early 20th century. Keynes contended that unemployment occurred because leakages exceeded injections, and therefore consumer demand was insufficient. The "cure" for unemployment was to prop up aggregate demand with fiscal policy efforts.

But, whether adjusting taxes (usually lowering them) or adjusting government spending (usually increasing it) is the best action to take is a matter of great political debate. Granted it is an oversimplification,

Republicans tend to favor reducing taxes to stimulate the economy, while Democrats, not necessarily opposed to lowered taxes, wish to include targeted government spending as part of an unemployment solution. The proper role of government is at the heart of the partisan controversy.

But, there is another camp called the Monetarists, perhaps best championed by Milton Friedman, an economist from the University of Chicago, who contended the controlling factor in causing/curing unemployment (and inflation, for that matter) was the money supply. In this situation, if the money supply expanded, and people were holding balances to suit their requirements, people would not wish to hold the extra funds and would spend them. Aggregate demand would thereby increase. So, the Federal Reserve System should use its tools to make the necessary increase in the country's money supply.

The truth is, of course, that there is truth in both views, and most modern economists believe that the properly controlling the nation's money supply is the better strategy for "long term" solutions, while fiscal policy can be effective when dealing with short term and/or emergency circumstances.

INFLATION BASICS

Students tend to readily understand the rather self-evident negative consequences of unemployment, but the evils of inflation are usually less clear. It acts like a hidden tax that reduces one's purchasing power, and once infected, it can be quite difficult to rid the economy of the "disease." So, we need to become better aware of its causes and preventions, if not cures.

What is inflation?

Inflation is all about the level of prices in a country, and, specifically, inflation occurs when the prices in general rise sustainably over a period of time, typically a year. As prices rise persistently, consumers are certainly disgruntled that they cannot afford to buy as many goods as before, but those on fixed incomes (e.g. retirees living on Social Security and/or pension sums) get even more alarmed. What is the typical response of a consumer when the price of something, say gasoline, shoots up? If you can buy less of it, that's fine. But, if the demand for the product is inelastic, such as gasoline, most consumers will seek to shave expenses by purchasing less (or none) of something else. That's difficult enough, but what can the citizen do when the prices of all goods, in general, are rising? And, again, what can those on fixed incomes do to try to keep up with the rising prices? Furthermore, if prices keep rising persistently, how should consumers and businesses plan their purchases and investments? Indeed, people have an incentive to save/invest less and spend now, but doing so only adds the inflationary pressures.

So, inflation distorts normal financial mechanisms and incentives; it is a serious economic problem to avoid and/or resolve.

How do we know inflation exists? How do we measure price levels?

Without pursuing more details that we need (though you are of course encouraged to research the topic in more depth), inflation is estimated by the Consumer Price Index (C.P.I.). This economic index measures the prices of a typical consumer's basket of goods and services:

> The CPIs are based on prices of food, clothing, shelter, and fuels, transportation fares, charges for doctors' and dentists' services, drugs, and other goods and services that people buy for day-to-day living. Prices are collected each month in 87 urban areas across the country from about 4,000 housing units and approximately 25,000 retail establishments-department stores, supermarkets, hospitals, filling stations, and other types of stores and service establishments. (BLS, 2010)

Once such measurements are compiled, the rate can be calculated as a percentage change from one time period to another. According to the Bureau of Labor Statistics below, the CPI for January of 2009 is 211.143, and the CPI for January of 2010 is 216.687. Hence, the inflation rate for 2009 was:

$$\frac{216.687 - 211.143}{211.143} = \frac{5.544}{211.143} = .026 = 2.6\%$$

There are excellent internet websites that can provide CPI indices and inflation rates for most any period; below are two graphs that depict the nation's inflation rates for 2000-2010:

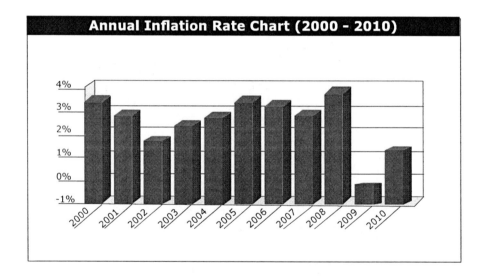

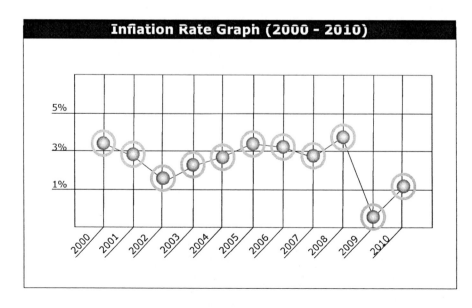

Us Inflation Calculator, 2010

YEAR	JAN.	FEB.	MAR.	APR.	MAY	JUN.	JUL.	AUG.	SEP.	OCT.	NOV.	DEC.	ANN.
2010	216.687	216.741	217.631	218.009	218.178	217.965	218.011	218.312	218.439	9999	9999	9999	9999
2009	211.143	212.193	212.709	213.24	213.856	215.693	215.351	215.834	215.969	216.177	216.33	215.949	214.537
2008	211.08	211.693	213.528	214.823	216.632	218.815	219.964	219.086	218.783	216.573	212.425	210.228	215.303
2007	202.416	203.499	205.352	206.686	207.949	208.352	208.299	207.917	208.49	208.936	210.77	210.036	207.342
2006	198.3	198.7	199.8	201.5	202.5	202.9	203.5	203.9	202.9	201.8	201.5	201.8	201.6
2005	190.7	191.8	193.3	194.6	194.4	194.5	195.4	196.4	198.8	199.2	197.6	196.8	195.3
2004	185.2	186.2	187.4	188	189.1	189.7	189.4	189.5	189.9	190.9	191	190.3	188.9
2003	181.7	183.1	184.2	183.8	183.5	183.7	183.9	184.6	185.2	185	184.5	184.3	183.96
2002	177.1	177.8	178.8	179.8	179.9	180.1	180.7	181	181.3	181.3	181.3	180.9	179.88
2001	175.1	175.8	176.2	176.9	177.7	178	177.5	177.5	178.3	177.7	177.4	176.7	177.1
2000	168.8	169.8	171.2	171.3	171.5	172.4	172.8	172.8	173.7	174	174.1	174	172.2
1999	164.3	164.5	165	166.2	166.2	166.2	166.7	167.1	167.9	168.2	168.3	168.3	166.6

Bureau of Labor Statistics website, 2010

WHAT CAUSES INFLATION?

We know from prior chapters that prices that rise for certain products because of changes in either the demand or supply of that specific product. The price can rise because either the producer supplies less of the item, or consumers increase their interest in the item and demand rise more than the producer can supply. But, what causes prices, in general, to rise and keep rising?

Recall our earlier introductions to the Keynesian and Monetarist and views. Well, they're back. And, that, of course, means that the cause of inflation is controversial.

John Maynard Keynes focused on the circular flow of activity and the potential imbalances of leakages and injections. Before, when looking at unemployment, Keynes argued that leakages were greater than injections; hence, aggregate was insufficient and needed a boost. Nor, when looking at inflation, the opposite has occurred, namely that injections are greater than leakages so that aggregate demand is too high. How can that happen?

Demand-Pull Inflation: regards price increases caused by persistent increases in consumer demand.

Demand – Pull Inflation:

Demand- pull inflation occurs because excessive demand "pulls up" prices. For a Keynesian, this development could only occur after full employment is reached (if full employment had not yet been reached, then the extra demand would first cause firms to produce more and hire more workers before resorting to increasing prices), and when demand outstripped supplies (and production capacities), the natural consequence is an increase in prices.

What would cause an increase in aggregate demand? Take your pick:
• Increased government spending (e.g., war, social programs)
• Increased consumer spending (e.g., general confidence level, renewed interest in home ownership)
• Increased growth in money supply (e.g., low interest rates, government prints more money instead of raising taxes)
• Increased growth in U.S. exports (e.g., growth in foreign countries create demand for U.S. goods, depreciation of the exchange rate making U.S. goods cheaper and more in demand)

"DEMAND - PULL" INFLATION

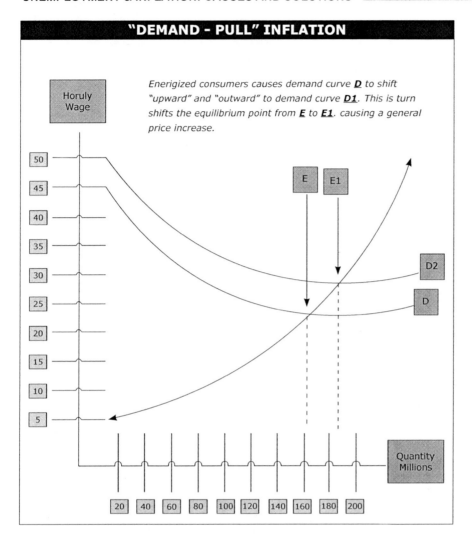

Enerigized consumers causes demand curve **D** to shift "upward" and "outward" to demand curve **D1**. This is turn shifts the equilibrium point from **E** to **E1**. causing a general price increase.

Cost-Push Inflation:

Cost-push inflation occurs when businesses experience causes that reduce production or make it more expensive. If the weather sends not enough rain (or too much rain) or sends too much heat (or not enough heat), crop failures mean that prices of the reduced supply will be higher. If the price of oil rises or labors are able to negotiate higher wages, then the costs of production are higher, and firms will either produce less (which will cause an increase in prices), or they will seek to cover those costs by raising their prices on their goods and services. (And, clearly, once inflation gets a foothold from any cause and workers started getting wage increases (called COLAs – Cost of Living Allowances), the pressures of rising prices causing rising wages causing more rising prices becomes a self-fulfilling spiral.)

Cost-Push Inflation: regards increase of price levels due to rising business costs.

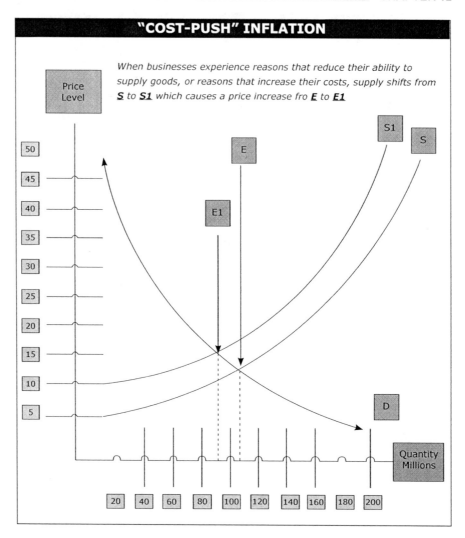

"COST-PUSH" INFLATION

When businesses experience reasons that reduce their ability to supply goods, or reasons that increase their costs, supply shifts from **S** to **S1** which causes a price increase fro **E** to **E1**

Price Level

Quantity Millions

Monetarists:

Dr. Friedman asserted that all economic problems were attributable to money supplies. Dr. Friedman is perhaps known for his resurgence of the Quantity Theory of Money (dating back to Copernicus) that says:

$$M \times V = P \times Y$$

where M = supply of money in circulation in a time period, say a year

where V = velocity of money, i.e. how many transactions occur in the time period,

where P = the price level

where Y = the quantity of real national output

In a very basic sense, the equation is saying that total spending (M x V) is equal to total revenues (P x Y), and the equation can be mathematically manipulated to show:

$$P = \frac{M \times V}{Y}$$

which asserts that price level equals the money supply times the velocity divided by the level of output.

Through empirical studies, Friedman proved that the velocity of money was rather constant, so if the output of goods and services also remained rather constant for a particular period of time, the only way for the national price level (P) to change was for the money supply (M) to change.

Hence, inflation was caused by an increase in the nation's money supply.

SOLUTIONS to INFLATION:

The matrix below pretty much covers the public policy strategies:

Fiscal Policy	Monetary Policy
The executive and legislative branches of the government can: 　　Raise taxes to give citizens less income to spend at their discretion	The Federal Reserve System can **decrease** the money supply by: raising the legal reserve requirement, raising the discount rate, and/or
Decrease government spending	selling bonds

CHAPTER SUMMARY

It should be reasonably obvious at this point that American capitalism can be a highly emotional topic. We place a philosophical preeminence on individual liberty, so our political and economic systems seek to maximize personal opportunity and responsibility and, therefore, minimize government intervention. Our legal as well as political and economic systems are constantly seeking to balance the rights and protections of the individual citizen and consumer with the needs of the common good. It should come as no surprise then that politicians with certain philosophical leanings will tend to gravitate toward economic solutions that are consistent with those leanings, and therefore, proposed strategies for resolving unemployment and/or inflation problems can become quite contentious. From a pragmatic standpoint, most modern politicians and economists tend to agree that the money supply should be kept a rather controlled amount, with nominal annual increases to accommodate GDP growth. The Fed can affect interest rates that can have a significant impact on either inflation or unemployment problems. But, politicians continue to use fiscal policy to impact aggregate demand, tough there is severe disagreement regarding whether lower taxes and/or targeted government spending is the appropriate solution to periods of unemployment. Politics. ☺

▶▶▌ *Chapter 12 Review*

Key concepts:

1. The United States labor force consists of all non-institutionalized individuals who are working or looking for work.

2. The unemployed are those who are not working, but who are actively looking for work; the unemployment rate is merely the number of unemployed divided by the labor force.

3. The federal government conducts a monthly Current Population Survey to estimate the extent of unemployment.

4. The U.S. labor force is undergoing a number of demographic changes, including a increased number of women and minorities as well as a general rise in the age of workers.

5. There are 4 categories of unemployment: a) frictional, 2) seasonal, 3) cyclical, and 4) structural.

6. The Minimum Wage is viewed as a potential solution to unemployment woes, but the public policy is quite controversial.

7. Fiscal policy can be used to address unemployment by lowering taxes to encourage citizens to spend the increased net income, by raising taxes for targeted government spending, and/or increased/targeted government spending to stimulate economic activity.

8. Monetary policy can lower interest rates and/or increase the money supply to facilitate increased economic activity.

9. Inflation regards sustained increase in prices throughout the economy; it is typically measured by the Consumer Price Index (CPI).

10. Inflation can be categorized as "Demand-Pull" or "Cost-Push" inflation.

11. Fiscal policy solutions to inflation are to raise taxes and/or curb government spending.

12. Monetary policy solutions regard increasing interest rates and/or decreasing the money supply.

Key terms:

labor force, unemployed, unemployment rate, frictional unemployment, cyclical unemployment, structural unemployment, minimum wage, inflation, CPI, Demand-Pull inflation, Cost-Push inflation, Quantity Theory of Money

CHAPTER 13

AMERICA'S 2008 FINANCIAL CRISIS

INTRODUCTION

While the seeds were sown as far back as the 1990's, the U.S. experienced a financial crisis during late (wasn't it late 2008?) early 2009 that many have called the worst since the Great Depression of the 1930's. Indeed, some economists nicknamed the event the "Great Recession." During this crisis, millions of Americans lost homes to foreclosure, over 8 million jobs were lost and unemployment reached nearly10%.

Thousands of businesses folded, well-known banks collapsed, Fannie Mae and Freddie Mac were seized, and the federal government made financial provisions (some called them bailouts) to the tune of $2.3 trillion to stem the tide.

What happened? While it is true that no economy is able to sustain growth every year, (recessions are part of economic cycles), and the U.S. has experienced dozens of recessions throughout its history, what made the 2008-2009 recession so "great"? And, of course, what caused it, and what measures can we take to seek to prevent it from occurring again?

Background – what happened and when

On Thursday September 18,2008, Fed Chairman Ben Bernanke met with Treasury Secretary Henry Paulson and key political legislators, and Bernanke reportedly advised those in the room that if the government didn't prepare a $700 billion emergency bailout, there might not be a recognizable economy by the following Monday. And, Treasury Secretary Paulson is alleged to have said, "Unless you act, the financial system of this country and the world will melt down in a matter of days" (PBS Frontline, 2010). The financial meltdown of 2008-2009 is special because of its unprecedented magnitude; no one seemed to be aware of the growing enormity of what later became known as "shadow banking," nor of just how powerful and interconnected our major financial institutions had become. As the events and analysis unfolded, Americans would repeatedly hear a new phrase: "Too Big to Fail." In many ways, this phrase summarized why this financial crisis was far different than those since the Great Depression.

LTCM: *is the investment bank that nearly started a financial crisis in the late 1990s.*

America actually experienced a foreshadowing of what was to come in the late 1990's.

Long Term Capital Management was an investment bank with over $125 billion in assets, mostly invested in hedge funds (unregulated mutual funds for the rich). LTCM had invested its customers' money in a variety of foreign investments including Russian bonds. In 1998 Russia announced that it had opted to devalue its currency and would default on paying its bond obligations. A significant segment of LTCM's portfolio was now worthless, and by late 1998 half of LTCM's asset value was lost. The problem was twofold. First, LTCM's short term liquidity was now in jeopardy, i.e., bankruptcy was a possibility. Second, many of the parties who had invested with LTCM were banks and pension/retirement funds, so LTCM's collapse would have devastating effects on millions of "innocent" Americans. In a similar emergency meeting, then FED Chairman Alan Greenspan and then Treasury Secretary Robert Rubin, alarmed that Long Term Capital Management might go bankrupt, convened a group of 14 bank CEO's and convinced them that it was in their long term interest to loan money to LTCM to provide a bail out. The bankers agreed and loaned LTCM $3.65 billion.

But, if we fast forward to 2008, a lot happened in those eight years that few, if any, had paid attention to. What happened is the escalation of what is called "shadow banking."

Recall from a prior chapter that our country had made a distinction between commercial banks, those that accepted deposits and, in turn, made loans to borrowers (for expanding a business, building or buying a home, taking a special vacation, etc.) and investment banks (that facilitated mergers and acquisitions, assisted with initial public offerings, and made investments for wealthy customers). The 1933 Glass Steagall legislation placed significant regulations on commercial banks, but no such restrictions on investment banks.

But, a basically successful financial history convinced policymakers to unwind many of the 1933 regulations; in 1982 President Reagan signed the Garn-St. Germain Depository Institutions Act that began the process of deregulation, and President Clinton signed the Gramm-Leach-Bliley Act of 1999 that repealed the parts of the Glass-Steagall Act that separated the distinctions between commercial and investment banks.

But, what politicians and regulators did not know was the exploding emergence of investment banking. After America's 9/11 tragedy and recession of 2001-2002, Alan Greenspan and the Fed opted to keep interest rates low to make borrowing easier and potential consumption high(er); that's rather standard strategy for battling a recession. But, at the same time interest rates were kept low, which also meant that interest sensitive investments like bonds would also yield low returns, a surplus of cash developed around the world, and investors went looking for investments with higher yields. So, investment banks created new investment products to seek to attract the excess cash; instruments called credit default swaps and collateralized debt obligations. And, since these investments were provided by investment banks – rather than traditional, commercial banks - these investments went unregulated. They even went unmonitored. Government officials were unaware of the volume of these transactions. Current Treasury Secretary, then FED Bank of New York President, Timothy Geithner best summarized the decade long development in his speech to the Economic Club of New York:

> The structure of the financial system changed fundamentally during the boom, with the dramatic growth in the share of assets outside the traditional banking system. The non-bank financial system grew to be very large, particularly in money and funding markets. In early 2007, asset-backed commercial paper conduits, in structured investment vehicles, in auction-rate preferred securities, tender options bonds and variable rate demand notes, had a combined asset size of roughly $2.2 trillion. Assets financed overnight in triparty repo grew to $2.5 trillion. Assets held in hedge funds grew to roughly $1.8trillion. The combined balance sheets of the then 5 major investment banks totaled $4 trillion.

> In comparison, the total assets of the top five bank holding companies in the United States at that point were just over $6 trillion, and the total assets of the entire banking system were about $10 trillion." (Geithner, 2008)

Notice, two developments were occurring simultaneously. First, unregulated investment banks were becoming a bigger and bigger percentage of America's financial industry, and, second, traditional banking (actually, banking in general), was being controlled by fewer and fewer banks. By 2010, we had an oligarchy; banking was (and still is) controlled by a handful of banking conglomerates: Goldman Sachs, Morgan Stanley, JP Morgan, Citigroup, Bank of America, and Wells Fargo.

Additionally, the general importance of the financial industry has consistently blossomed for the past 50 years. In 1945, America's financial industry was about 2.5% of our GDP and by 2000, the importance had grown to nearly 10%.

So, what was silently happening from 1999 to 2008 (and beyond) is that:

- banking was growing into a very substantial sector of our GDP
- unregulated investment banks were booming
- unregulated investment banks were booming because of new created, complex investment vehicles
- banking is being highly concentrated into a handful of banks

Lastly, what developed was a shocking change in moral consequence. Moral hazard gave way to systemic risk. What does that mean? Moral hazard is a time honored economic principle that says an economic system should not provide incentives to take excess risk and otherwise behave imprudently. If one takes a risk that does not work out, the economic consequence should be a financial loss to the risk-taker so as to teach him a lesson not to engage in such risky behavior again. The major criticism of a bail-out is that it fails to allow some economic loss to teach a lesson to the risk taker. But, since our financial activity has become so concentrated and inter-connected, the failure of one key bank or financial institution could have a rippling effect on another bank that could have a rippling effect on another bank, and on and on. Because the whole system has become so interdependent, especially on the 5-6 major banks, the whole banking system is at risk if 1-2 key players suffer from poor and/or greedy judgments. Because we have systemic risk, we can't teach anyone a lesson by allowing it to fail. There's no incentive to behave prudently if a bail-out will be needed to save the entire system.

Why Did it Happen?

Frustratingly, the 2008 U.S. Financial Crisis appears to have many parties to blame, and experts differ as to which is the "guiltiest." It may be true that one or two may be more dominant than the others, but it can just as easily be argued that the U.S. experienced a highly unusual convergence of 7-8 parties that manifested surprising apathy and/or substantial greed. (Parties include the Fed, homebuyers, mortgage brokers, appraisers, investment bankers, federal regulators, bond rating agencies, and even Congress/the White House.)

But, seeking to simplify matters a bit, we can reasonably group the causes and culprits into two connected developments that shocked our financial system: 1) the housing bubble (2003-2006), and 2) the meltdown of what is commonly called the shadow banking system (2007-2008).

We now know that at least some of the seeds for the subsequent crisis were sown by Alan Greenspan and the Federal Reserve back in 2003. America experienced a recession in 2001-2002, intensified by the dot.com bubble, the 9-11 tragedy, corporate scandals (Enron, WorldCom, Adelphia, Tyco, et al), and the invasion of Iraq Subsequently, the Fed opted to keep interest rates lower than necessary in 2003-2005 to help facilitate a faster recovery.

However, the mortgage lending industry now had a very cheap source of money; mortgage rates lowered, so the demand for housing increased. (It was also true that there was a "global glut" of savings in search of investments, so the United States had also received an influx of foreign investment dollars that helped provide lots of mortgage money for homes.) Since home ownership is essentially subsidized by the IRS tax code, coupled with some government programs to assist home ownership in certain neighborhoods of most U.S. cities (e.g. the George H.W. Bush administration lowered the regulation of Fannie Mae and Freddie Mac by lowering their capital reserve requirements; the Clinton Administration urged Fannie Mae to expand mortgage loans to low and middle income Americans, and the George W. Bush Administration created a variety of home ownership subsidies to facilitate mortgages for low income home buyers). Therefore, an interest in home ownership surged which had the net effect of increasing housing prices year after year. A bubble was born.

This persistent increase in housing prices was a blessing to lenders (if a borrower began to have trouble with his loan, he could just sell the property at a higher price to someone else), and the bubble created an incentive for purchasers to purchase as quickly as possible. (This is "Demand-Pull" inflation at work.) These incentives caused loan applicants to seek loan amounts they could not afford, and in some cases, they provided false income information so as to qualify for the loan package.

On the other side of the table, lenders offered as many creative loan arrangements as they could to get loans approved; that's when Americans began to hear words like "subprime" and "ARM", i.e. adjustable rate mortgage. (Incredibly, Countrywide, the nation's largest mortgage lender at the time, announced its policy that down payments would no longer be required. Countrywide, sued by the State of California for unscrupulous practices, later was seized by the Office of Thrift Supervision when housing prices fell and new home owners, facing rising ARM payments and unable to refinance, began defaulting. Countrywide was later acquired by Bank of America in January, 2008.)

With ample monies available for mortgages and an influx of prospective home buyers, lenders went on a lending frenzy. Lenders received large bonuses for every mortgage they closed, and few were concerned about whether the borrower could truly afford the mortgage; with housing prices in a persistent rise, any applicant could always sell his home to another at a profit if it turned out he could not handle the loan. Additionally, the mortgage lender quickly sold the mortgage to another party, so the mortgage company had no vested interest in whether the borrower could actually afford the loan in the long run. As some said, brokers had no long term "skin in the game." And, sadly, one must add that many appraisers got caught up in the mania and incorrectly valued property to help facilitate loan applications that should never have been approved.

The net result was tens of thousands of approved mortgages that the borrowers could not ultimately afford. (And, frustratingly, the subsequent recession caused layoffs, which in turn caused financial dilemmas for other homeowners (who could afford their mortgages, assuming continued employment). These layoffs have increased the number of foreclosures and loan defaults.)

Against this backdrop of a housing boom, financial institutions, especially investment banks, and many foreign investors, including foreign governments, were looking for investments that could earn higher yields than the current, modest rates of return. Hence, a "flood of funds", some domestic and some foreign, reached the American financial markets at about the same time as the housing boom. And, investment banks proceeded to create complex investment vehicles for their individual and institutional customers: MBS (mortgage backed security) and CDS (credit default swap) instruments.

Freddie Mac and Fannie Mae: are government sponsored enterprises that assist banks and brokers to provide affordable mortgages.

Mortgage-backed securities have been in existence for a long time, but they were mostly used by the government established Federal National Mortgage Association, (FNMA) (Fannie Mae) and the Federal Home Loan Mortgage Corporation, i.e. FHLMC (Freddie Mac). Fannie Mae and Freddie Mac would purchase mortgages created by small(er) banks, mortgage companies, and other loan originators, pool them, and then sell them to institutional investors. The purpose of the entities was to facilitate mortgages to low and middle income home buyers by purchasing the mortgages from the loan originator. Then, the spent funds would be recouped by selling a pool of mortgages to investors. This maneuver would also guarantee that the investors would receive their anticipated monthly stream of payments. Hence, while there was some risk that low and/or middle income home buyers would subsequently be unable to pay their mortgage, the government sponsored enterprise (Fannie Mae or Freddie Mac) was on the hook. The loan originator had its mortgage paid off when Fannie Mae or Freddie Mac bought it. While institutional investors then purchased a group of mortgages, their monthly stream of mortgage payments was guaranteed. If a mortgagor stopped paying, Fannie Mae or Freddie Mac would. (While government "sponsored," Fannie Mae and Freddie Mac were private, profit enterprises, so they made payments on bad mortgages from their profits. Because of their continued payments, they were not a drag on U.S. taxpayers.)

However, lots of investment banks wanted a piece of the booming mortgage action, so they started to compete with Fannie Mae and Freddie Mac in buying the mortgages that mortgage lenders and small(er) banks had originated. In 2004, the Securities and Exchange Commission relaxed the capital requirements for investment banks that enabled investment banks to leverage their funds even more and create more investment products, including MBS's. (Remind reader of what an "MBS" is)

So, for example, Bank A buys a pool of mortgages, say 5,000. (Securitization means that the risk of a defaulted loan is lessened when combined with lots of other similar loans.) Now Bank A can package these 5,000 mortgages into groups, say 500 mortgages per group, and sell a group (called a tranche, which is the French word for slice) of mortgages to an individual and/or institutional investor who wants the monthly stream of mortgage payments. The pricing of these groupings is what gets dicey since not all mortgages carry the same risk. Bank A could conceivably package the better mortgages and sell them at a higher price to investors, and package lower grade mortgages to be sold to investors at a lower price. This selling of slices at different prices is CDO (collateral debt obligation) securitization).

Of course, Bank A may very well have sold some groupings, aka some tranches, to other financial institutions, say Bank B and Bank C that, in turn, opted to later sell some of their mortgages to yet other investors, including Bank D and Bank E. And, since the banking industry was deregulated back in the 1980's and 1990's, the last two decades have seen many of our banks become huge trading rooms where securities are bought and sold for profit.

So, by 2007-2008, Wall Street financial institutions wound up with billions (trillions?) of dollars of unregulated "mortgage backed securities" that had been purchased in bundles from originating mortgage companies and then "traded" among themselves. And, what those institutional investors didn't realize was that a significant portion of those mortgage bundles contained "toxic" mortgages.

Derivatives: are insurance instruments to hedge risk.

But, let's not get ahead of ourselves since MBS's are only one of the two problem products. We now need to turn our attention to credit default swaps.

A credit default swap is a form of insurance and it is part of the family of financial products called derivatives. Derivatives are financial contracts that help mitigate against risk; i.e., hedge. Derivative contracts are often used quite appropriately in commodity trading where a

Credit Default Swap: is an instrument to transfer the credit risk to another party.

farmer and a miller each want to reduce future risk. So, for instance, the farmer and the miller may agree to a contract in which the farmer will sell a specific amount of the commodity (e.g. corn) to the miller for a specific amount of money. The farmer now knows he can count on a particular amount of revenue, and the miller is expecting to receive a certain volume of product.

A credit default swap is one type of a derivative product. Often, CDS's are bought and sold over bonds. A bond is a fancy "I.O.U." in which the purchaser of the bond agrees to give the seller of the bond a pre-determined sum of cash, say $1,000, and the bond seller agrees to pay back the sum plus an agreed upon amount of interest at a specified future date (when the bond matures). Say, in a year, the bond seller agrees to pay the bond holder $1,100. (Hence, the extra $100 is the interest amount, which represents an interest rate of 10%.)

But, there are two risks associated with purchasing a bond. First, interest rates can fluctuate, so after purchasing a bond, the buyer "loses" if interest rates, in general, rise because the purchaser has locked up those funds at a lower rate. Second, there's no guarantee that the bond seller will remain solvent to pay the bond (IOU) when it matures.

Holders of bonds then wish to reduce the risk of their investments by purchasing insurance against the possibility of a default by the bond seller. And, credit default swaps fit that need. When purchasing a CDS, the bondholder is "swapping" the risk of default with another party who will pay the bondholder in the event of a bankruptcy (or default) of the bond seller. Like any other insurance product, the purchaser of a credit default swap pays a premium to the CDS seller in exchange for payment if a default occurs. The common time frame for a CDS contract is 5 years.

It was actually JP Morgan Bank that began (promoted?) the Credit Default Swap craze. In the mid 1990's, JP Morgan was experiencing every bank's frustration; it had made tens of billions of dollars in loans to various solid customers, but by federal law was required to hold a percentage of that asset value in capital reserves in the event that a few of the loans went sour. Hence, the bank was sitting on a huge amount of "idle" cash. What to do. What to do. If there were only a way to "guarantee" those loans, that could free up the capital just sitting around in reserve. Then they could make even more money. You guessed it. While the concept was already in existence, theoretically, JP Morgan created a Swap Desk and seriously created a market for these loan "guarantees."

However, CDS's are not regulated, so there's both an oddity and a problem associated with them. First, the oddity is that one may buy a CDS contract even though one has nothing to do with the asset that the contract concerns. In law, that's called an insurable interest. (You cannot buy a life insurance policy on someone you don't know because you have no insurable interest in the outcome.) Risk speculators could now "invest" in assets they didn't own or in situations they were not party to. For instance, if you begin to believe that Company A is in trouble and won't be able to pay its obligations, you can speculate by buying credit default swaps on Company A's bonds, believing that Company A will not get the bonds repaid, and therefore you will get paid by the CDS insurance contract. Or, consider the reverse: if you think Company A is in great financial shape, you might sell CDS insurance contracts to others who have the opposite viewpoint. Credit default swaps are just bi-lateral, private agreements between two parties who want to bet on the outcome of a situation they aren't really otherwise part of.

Second, the problem with CDS's is that, with such limited experience with them, pricing them was true speculation. And, again, because there was no regulation, sellers of credit default swaps may or may not have held enough capital in reserve to pay off claims should they occur.

So, soon, financial institutions were not just buying and selling mortgage-backed securities (pools of mortgages that had been bought, then "sliced", then sold again), but were buying and selling credit default swaps to hedge various other investments that the institution had made.

But, now, financial institutions were tethered together by all of the inter-connected contracts, whose values were ultimately dependent upon Americans paying their mortgages.

So, the meltdown began when the financial arrangements made in 2003-2007 mortgages turned, and either home buyers were not able to refinance (as promised) or home-owners suddenly discovered they had an adjustable rate mortgage (ARM) and could not afford the new, higher rate. And, because the bubble had burst, housing prices stopped rising and the demand for home ownership cooled off, the troubled home-owners also could not sell the home to someone else at a price higher than they paid. Suddenly, thousands could not pay their mortgage.

And, when thousands of Americans stopped paying their mortgages, that meant some of the mortgages in those packages of mortgage back securities (an asset to the purchaser) weren't worth what the financial institution (often an investment bank) paid to acquire them. And, as time continued, a "sour" mortgage became worth less and less with the home-owner making no mortgage payment, and then more home-owners began not paying on their mortgage. Hence, most of our large financial institutions had assets (MBS investments) on their books whose true value now became a total mystery. Certainly the MBS investment was declining in value, but declining down to what? There was no bottom in sight as

Lehman Brothers: is the investment bank that went bankrupt due to excessive risk taking.

foreclosures only increased and increased in 2007 and 2008. Hence, anticipated bank revenues declined, and no one could be sure what the mortgage based investments were truly worth.

AIG: is a very large insurance company that nearly went bankrupt from its involvement in derivatives.

Then, as financial institutions became unable to meet their bond obligations, many of those credit default swap "investments" kicked in, and companies who had sold such contracts needed to pay claims. Financial institutions who sold a lot of CDS contracts were headed for bankruptcy. The chain of event went like this: The CDS seller had sold lots more contracts that it ever expected to have to pay and/or it didn't price its CDS contracts well and didn't receive enough premium revenue in the first place. The sellers didn't keep enough of a capital reserve on hand to pay claims, if necessary.

And, this is exactly what happened to Bear Stearns, Lehman Brothers, and AIG. Bear Stearns and Lehman Brothers were huge investment banks, and AIG was a traditional insurance company that opted to pursue the CDS market, and all three got caught in liquidity problems. They didn't have enough revenue and liquid assets to pay their financial obligations.

(If you recall your history, Bear Stearns got a government bailout, although the bailout was merely a buyout by JP Morgan facilitated by a guaranteed government loan should it be needed. Lehman Brothers was allowed to go bankrupt, and AIG received a government bailout of tens of millions of dollars which has since been repaid.)

The government and others probably first became aware of the "emergency crisis" when it became clear that Bear Stearns was in financial trouble. Bear had purchased hundreds of thousands of sub-prime mortgages, bundled them into MBS's and sold them to investors. Additionally, Bear had sold credit default swaps to its investors; these contracts were worth "hundreds of billions of dollars all over Wall Street and around the world" (PBS Frontline, 2010). While still a huge bank by banking standards, Bear was also the smallest of the major investment Wall Street banks, and rumors began to swirl that Bear was in financial trouble and would not be able to pay its obligations. And, therefore, no other bank would lend it money for fear of throwing good money after bad.

(In May of 2008 the government ultimately facilitated a buyout of Bear Stearns by JP Morgan.)

This event sparked (or confirmed, depending upon one's point of view) a bank run on investment banks. Bank runs are largely a thing of the past for traditional, commercial banks because the Federal Deposit Insurance Corporation (FDIC) insures every deposit account up to $250,000 per account, so even if one's local bank goes bankrupt, your funds are still guaranteed. (Admittedly, depositors won't want to wait for their funds to be "returned" by the FDIC. The process takes time, so if rumors are real and persistent, there can still be a run by some depositors who hope to withdraw all of their funds before the bank is actually seized.) But, investment banks are not regulated so they don't have a similar safety net for their customers. The only recourse for an investment bank to stop a run is to persuade the public that it has plenty of funds and there is no need to panic. The CEO usually makes some sort of press announcement in the hope of alleviating any rumors, and behind the scenes a bank actually in trouble will seek to get a loan to weather the storm.

But, because nearly all of the major banks were inter-connected with these "toxic assets" and no one knew for sure who was solvent and who wasn't, banks stopped lending. They wouldn't lend to one another, nor would they lend to businesses because no bank was willing to risk its existing capital; everyone needed every penny to meet current obligations. What if it became the target of a rumor and a bank run? It would need every penny it already had. And, if it lent out funds to another bank, what if it became a bank run target? Would the lending bank get it money back? As Nobel prize-winning economist Paul Krugman wrote,

> What lies behind the credit squeeze is the combination of reduced trust in and decimated capital at financial institutions. People and institutions, including the financial institutions, don't want to deal with anyone unless they have substantial capital to back up their promises, yet the crisis has depleted capital across the board. (Return of Depression Economics, 2009)

Therefore, in a nutshell, the bursting housing bubble created "toxic assets" (mortgage backed securities with declining values, and credit default swaps that sellers were unprepared to pay), and because Wall Street banks were so inter-connected, a lending freeze ensued once a bank run on investment banks developed. That credit freeze spilled over into commercial lending so that businesses couldn't borrow for normal business operations, and consumers, watching the news, became nervous about job security and started to reduce their normal spending. The whole mess spiraled downward into a recession, The Great Recession of 2008-2009. We are still digging our way out.

So, who's the culprit in all of this? Take your pick:

1) 2003 Fed decision to keep interest rates (too) low
2) Incentives for home ownership
   a) Tax code rewards home ownership
   b) SEC and Fannie Mae changes reduce capital requirements
   c) Government assistance programs for low income buyers
3) Mortgage lending and appraisal practices

       a)   Ignorant/fraudulent home buyers

       b)   Unethical/fraudulent lending practices

       c)   Excessive bonuses to brokers to "get a deal done"

       d)   Shady appraisals

    4)   Poor rating performance by Moody's and Standard & Poor's

    5)   Lack of needed regulation

       a)   Glass-Steagall distinctions rescinded

       b)   Shadow banking significantly increases

    6)   Excessive risk taking

       a)   Mortgage backed security practices (e.g. collateralized debt obligations

       b)   Credit default swap contracts

Solutions (financial and Wall Street reforms)

Ok. Now what? How can this mess be cleaned up and prevented?

Cleaning up the problem is not particularly controversial in theory; we must first "unfreeze" the credit markets and get money flowing again through loans – appropriate loans – need to start happening again. That simply means that banks must have confidence restored, and that occurs by infusing more money into the credit markets. There's only one party who can do that at this point: government. Call it a bailout, call it a loan, call it whatever you wish, but the solution to a bank run and the re-building of confidence is an infusion of money so parties stop worrying that there won't be enough.

Politicians argued about how best to unfreeze the lending markets, but the Fed ultimately both pumped more money into the economy and "bought" some toxic assets from banks so they didn't have to worry about them.

A second necessary step was/is to stimulate the economy out of the severe recession that had been created by the crisis. Alarmingly, of course, the Wall Street crisis "spilled over" into a main street crisis causing consumers to drastically cut back on their spending which only served to cause layoffs when businesses didn't sell as much. Recessions are at the heart a problem of insufficient consumer demand (not enough consumer spending). The devil is almost always in the details, so while there was great political debate and disagreement, President Obama and a majority of Congress members pushed a Stimulus Package that offered nearly a trillion dollars of tax cuts, grants to state governments, and spending projects, all designed to prevent more layoffs, stop the GDP decline, and build momentum to slowly increase spending and confidence levels of consumers and businesses. Partisan criticism continues even today: Some economists say the stimulus wasn't *large enough*; members of one of the political parties say there should have been *no stimulus at all*.

The third step, regulatory reform of the financial industry, was first proposed in 2009 by outgoing Senator Christopher Dodd (D-CT), and the 1,336 page Restoring American Financial Stability Act of 2010 had great promise. Lots of regulations are probably needed:

1) requiring 10% down payments by prospective homebuyers

2) requiring mortgage companies to maintain ownership of mortgages for a minimum of 3-5 years

3) requiring banks to hold larger capital reserves

4) requiring shadow banking transactions be done in public exchanges

5) making private CDS contract unenforceable if the buyer has no insurance interest in the market.

We could list many, many more, but the final legislation was hammered out in conference between a House bill passed in December of 2009 and a Senate version passed in May of 2010. Details were finalized in the 2,300 page Dodd-Frank Wall Street Reform and Consumer Protection Act signed on July 21, 2010.

Among other features, the legislation created two new agencies, Financial Stability Oversight Council and the Bureau of Consumer Financial Protection.

Consumer Protection: act regarding legislation designed to provide financial regulatory reform.

The Consumer Financial Protection Bureau (CFPB) was the brainchild of then Harvard law professor Elizabeth Warren (now a U.S. Senator representing Massachusetts) who advocated the need for improved governmental oversight to educate and protect American consumers from deceptive as well as illegal practices by banks, mortgage lenders, and other financial institutions. Political critics blocked her nomination/confirmation, so Ohio Attorney General Rich Cordray became the agency's first director. The CFPB officially began in January, 2012.

Its critics alleged that the Consumer Financial Protection Bureau was both unnecessary (consumers should generally be more responsible, if not cautious) and a potentially stifling watch dog (imposing unrealistic or even counter productive regulations), but the agency's website shares that its mission is "to make markets for consumer financial products and services work for Americans – whether they are applying for a mortgage, choosing among credit cards, or using any number of other consumer financial products."

It may be years before we know the full impact of the Dodds-Frank legislation, but all signs pointed to the following:

1. Because the U.S. wound up with a patchwork of banking laws, regulations, and regulatory bodies, a representative body

of "systemic risk" evaluators will be created to coordinate needed regulator controls. We need one body, not dozens, with meaningful authority to set policy

2. A new consumer protection division will be created (probably with the Federal Reserve System) to write and enforce rules to prevent predatory lending practices by mortgage companies

3. Give regulators the power to oversee the derivatives market; require such investments to be handled through a third party, (exchanges which will make such contracts open and transparent), and a final bill may require investment banks to create separate corporate divisions of any derivatives business operations, i.e. proprietary trading will be separated from the traditional business of banking

4. Create both a fund (paid for by banks) and a process (written by governmental regulators) to "unwind" a financial institution that is heading for bankruptcy; one bank's failure should not "take down" the whole system, and taxpayers should not be paying for any "emergency bailout" or bankruptcy process.

Regulation of the economy for any reason is the essence of public policy which is where economic and politics intersect. Fireworks almost always result. So, students are urged to research the final provisions of the financial reform legislation that was passed in the summer of 2010. See if the strategies make good sense to you.

CHAPTER SUMAMARY

The U.S. Financial Crisis of 2007-2008 has been labeled as the biggest financial "disaster" since the 1930's Great Depression. According to the Secretary of the Treasury under outgoing President George Bush and the new Secretary of the Treasury under incoming President Barak Obama, the country was headed over a cliff into a financial abyss of unchartered territory. While there are any number of culprits, who were guilty of unbridled greed and/or apathetic ignorance, it now seems rather clear that the crisis began in the housing market, where thousands, if not tens of thousands, of "toxic" mortgages were created and then sold in bundles to banks who sold them as investments to other banks who sold them to ….. As people began to default on the mortgage, the value of such an asset declined, and banks began to develop cash flow problems that caused fears about the solvency of a variety of investment parties, including most of America's major banks. When a few of those major banks actually did need to file for bankruptcy, a "panic" gripped the financial system so that lending all but froze. Consumers became fearful and dramatically reduced spending habits, so the combination of declining consumer spending and frozen credit markets caused businesses to lay off workers to prevent their bankruptcy, and the cycle began to feed off itself. We entered into a serious, lengthy recession. And, while the recession may be technically over as of this writing, the nation's unemployment rate still hovers near 9% (not true) (and is much higher in many pockets throughout the country).

Amidst significant partisan politics, President Obama and the Democratic controlled House and Senate passed legislation to stop additional layoffs and economic decline, and the legislation sought to stimulate economic recovery with a package of tax cuts and targeted government spending. Political bickering about the details of the "stimulus bill" continue to this day.

Additionally, though slightly less contentious, President Obama and the Democratic controlled House and Senate also passed financial reform legislation to reign in Wall Street practices, protect consumers from unscrupulous lenders, and devise future regulations to address any need to "unwind" a bank "too big to fail" without a need of a taxpayer bailout. Again, political controversies about this legislation continue to this day.

This economic event in America's history confirms how intertwined economics and politics are in the U.S.

(Are you not going to mention Elizabeth Warren and the Consumer Protection Financial Bureau?)

▶▶❙ *Chapter 13 Review*

Key concepts:

1. America's financial crisis in 2007-2008 was the worst financial decline since the Great Depression of the 1930's.

2. The seeds of the crisis were sown up to a decade earlier, including factors such as the development of "shadow banking," risky investments such as derivatives, low interest rates, and questionable mortgage practices.

3. Hence, there were many culprits that contributed to the economic meltdown, including the unwinding of banking regulations, the Fed's decision to keep interest rate low, tax code incentives for home ownership, shady lending practices and greedy mortgage applicants, apathetic appraisal and rating agency performances, and excessive risk-taking by Wall Street banks.

4. As mortgage foreclosures began to appear and increase, bank investments became questioned, and a financial "panic" froze credit markets. Consumer apprehension caused a decline in consumer spending, and (small) businesses

were unable to secure routine loans; both created layoffs and a rising unemployment. Confidence was shaken and the economy was a self-fulfilling downward spiral.

5. The federal government opted to loan funds to major banks to prevent more bank failures, and the federal government opted to stimulate economic activity via tax cuts and targeted spending.

6. Congress also passed financial reform legislation to re-impose some banking regulations as well as create new agencies to better monitor banks and protect consumers from predatory lending practices.

Key terms:

Long Term Capital Management, Fannie Mae and Freddie Mac, Commodity Futures Trading Commission, Countrywide, derivatives, credit default swaps, Lehman Brothers, AIG, Consumer Protection Act of 2010

CHAPTER 14

THE GROWING INCOME GAP

An individual's annual income can be determined by several factors, and those various factors can cause a variety of different outcomes for individual financial success. Often, those with an official education are paid more than those without an education, employees with greater experience and/or skill will usually command higher compensation, and some are just more diligent and hard-working than others. Some work in difficult or risky circumstances, and some work hours that most would rather be asleep. And, yes, some just happen to be in the right place at the right time, and some have connections to the right people. When viewed honestly, few would advocate that everyone deserves the same financial outcome as everyone else as most Americans believe that there should be some general correlation between merit and financial achievement. Hence, different levels of merit (diligence, education, and skill) will cause different income outcomes.

But, of course, while there can be millions of Americans falling into different economic levels, a goal of our economic system is to increase the Gross Domestic Product so that the general economic growth improves the financial lot for most everyone in the country. Politicians are fond of saying, "a rising tide lifts all boats", which means that a solidly improving economy will create opportunities for most to increase their standard of living. Prosperity throughout the U.S. has been a long-term upward trend of continued expansion (the DJIA has risen from around 1,000 to 13,000 over the last 35 years), with the decade of the 1990's being especially favorable for sustained growth: unemployment, welfare and poverty rates all fell, and incomes grew for just about all Americans.

However, while incomes should never be equal, America's gap between the "haves" and the "have-nots" has never been greater, and that gap has steadily widened for the last 15-20 years. Indeed, America's financial crisis of 2007-2008 has actually served to unearth just how "jaw-dropping" the increase in income inequality has become. For example, just in the 5 year span of 2002 to 2007, 65% of America's wealth was held by the top 1% of our citizenry (Freeland, 2011). If such a trend continues, the U.S. is likely to face social consequences that could threaten the cohesion and unity of the country. If you are a fan of a healthy "middle class" (as I am), then the issue deserves our attention.

History of Income Inequality

When economists, startled by the rising inequality, began looking back at the origins of the middle-class America, they discovered to their surprise that the transition from the inequality of the Gilded Age to the relative equality of the postwar era wasn't a gradual evolution. Instead, America's postwar middle-class society was *created*, in just a space of a few years, by the policies of the Roosevelt administration – especially through wartime wage controls. The economic historians Claudia Goldin and Robert Margo, who first documented this surprising reality, dubbed it the Great Compression. Now, you might have expected inequality to spring back to its former levels once wartime controls were removed. It turned out, however, that the relatively equal distribution of income created by FDR persisted for more than thirty years. This strongly suggests that institutions, norms, and the political environment matter a lot more for the distribution of income – and that impersonal market forces matter less – than Economics 101 might lead you to believe. (Krugman, 2007)

Professor Krugman's quotation is useful for at least two reasons, the first of which I want to cover right at the outset: America has experienced a "long" roller coaster ride of income movement in which we propelled from income inequality to relative equality and now back to inequality. Let's trace that propulsion. (The second point is that income "equality" can be politically developed; we'll discuss that notion later in the chapter.)

Pre-1900 America was essentially a society of the privileged and everyone else. For many Americans, living conditions were challenging and there were no social services as we have today. While statistics are hard to come by, anecdotal evidence indicates that the 1800's was a time of vast inequality of power and, therefore, wealth. But, we do know, for instance, that labor laws were all but non-existent prior to the New Deal era, and history is replete with examples of employee abuse, even towards minors. Any attempts by employees to organize into any sort of labor union met with legal repression; strikes were met with authorized physical violence. And, we know that the number of billionaires at the turn of the century and into the Roaring Twenties was actually higher than the number of billionaires in the 1960's. Indeed, the Sherman Anti-trust Act, passed in 1890, was a signal that the fortunes made by the robber barons were getting out of hand. Still, government was small (public administration and bureaucracy weren't discovered and used much until the 1920's), so the laissez-faire atmosphere created a "survival of the fittest" mindset that benefited the few against the deprivations of the many. Admittedly, every American's plight improved as the country grew from post Civil War to World War I, and 20th Century America was far richer than most other countries around the world, but disparity between the elite and everyone else was real, and it was real big.

A solid political text will outline the reasons for the history we just noted, but our focus here is that the economic consequences began to change in the early 1900's. Actually, some seeds were sown across the Atlantic when Europeans began to establish some safety net programs (e.g. Germany introduced old-age pensions in the 1880's and Great Britain adopted old-age insurance and a health insurance program in 1910-1911), but it was the Great Depression of the 1930's that finally convinced America that changes were necessary. (To be fair, the political debate rages on to this day regarding whether such changes were necessary or effective, but most economists across the political spectrum acknowledge that the "turning point" for creating a new trend line, in this case, with income inequality, was the Great Depression.) In short, the Great Depression was the catalyst for what politicians call the New Deal, and the New Deal began what Goldin and Margo labeled as the Great Compression, that is, the inequality gap began to contract.

Why? What happened? In a word: government. While it is believed that no one especially defended the growing income inequality from 1870 (post Civil War) through the 1920's (post World War I) , many thought there wasn't anything anyone could do about it, and inefficient, wasteful government was most assuredly not capable of making it better. In a sense, President Roosevelt was "lucky" in that the economic crisis of the Great Depression as well as the subsequent national security upheaval of World War II allowed him to convince a majority of Americans that increased governmental involvement in their lives was the only real option. While there were plenty of critics (just as there are today), Americans were willing to give "big government" a chance; indeed, the survival of the country's future might be at stake.

In hindsight, the "creation" of a burgeoning middle class (from around 1945 through 1980's) was the result of four government interventions. First, during wartime, the government's National War Labor Board controlled wages. (President Nixon would later take the extraordinary step of freezing wages in an attempt to control inflation.)

The measure may seem surprising or even un-American to you, but difficult times call for difficult measures, and the NWRB often made wage decisions that "lifted" wages for low income employees and/or "limited" wage levels for high(er) income employees. These labor board decisions were often used as benchmarks for wage and salary judgments throughout affected industries.

Second, labor was finally given a chance to meaningfully organize. Admittedly, labor unions can get just as greedy or even just as violent as employers, and unionized labor peaked at about 25% of the American labor force during this 40 year period, so unionized labor has never been a major part of America's labor force. But, labor unions did negotiate contracts, quite peacefully and quite routinely most of the time, helping to-raise the income levels and standards of living of millions of American workers.

Third, the beginnings of what came to be known as the "safety net" occurred during this period. The federal government enacted what was then a modest Social Security program and a Medicare Health Insurance program for the elderly, and states began to pass legislation that provided some income benefits for work-related injuries. A more comprehensive workers compensation program would later be developed.

Fourth, the politicians made no bones about it; they taxed the wealthy. Income tax rates on the upper income classes rose from 25% to 65%, and the rate reached as high as 90% during President Eisenhower's tenure. Additionally, the corporation income tax also rose from about 15% to around 45%, and the inheritance taxes were raised to make it more difficult for the rich to pass on their wealth to their heirs. In 1929, America's top 1% owned 20% of the country's wealth, but that percentage had dropped to 10% by the 1950's. (Krugman, 2007)

Lastly, it was during these "golden years" that many employers began providing fringe benefits to employees. Health insurance coverage was affordable and the more forward-thinking firms were offering retirement plans to encourage employee loyalty.

Political and philosophical debates abounded (and they still do), but work initiative was not destroyed, businesses continued to invest in America's future, wage demands did not collapse capitalism, and the social fabric, while far from perfect (racial discrimination was still a major blemish on America's image as the land of opportunity), was never more harmonious and unified. America had a legitimate middle class in which real income for a family doubled from about $22,000 to $44,000 (in today's price index), most owned a car, and the vast majority had a telephone. Though some families drove a luxury car while many drove a compact, the differences among the lifestyles had drastically diminished. For the first time in our history, the majority of American families could be considered as belonging to the middle class.

Today's Data

The pendulum has already been swinging back to the inequalities of the pre-New Deal era. One telling example is illustrated by two major American employers of their day: General Motors was America's big name employer in the 1960's. They paid their workers about $50,000 a year in wages and fringe benefits (in today's dollars), while Wal-Mart, America's big name employer in the 21st century, pays its employees an average of $17,000 a year (Reich, 2007). While America's GDP continues to grow, the wealth is hardly spreading across all income classes. In the 1980's economists were beginning to see that a small minority of Americans were pulling farther and farther ahead while the rest pretty much tread water.

Unemployment was (only) 4.5% in 2007 and corporate profits were the highest percentage of the economy's GDP since the Great Depression, yet polls indicated that just 33% of the population thought the economic conditions were "good" or "excellent." With such general prosperity, why were a majority of Americans unimpressed with the progress of the 1990's and first decade of the new millennium? The answer, I believe, is that while the overall numbers for the aggregate economy were steadily increasing, the gains were not hitting ordinary Americans; they felt no better off, and indeed many were less well off than their parents.

In 2010, President Obama and the Congress created a new agency, the Consumer Financial Protection Bureau, to help address the growing hole in the nations' economic boat. Elizabeth Warren, tapped to head the agency, shared in a CBS News interview,

> We have a problem that's been underway for 30 years, of squeezing, chipping, hitting on the middle class – flat wages, rising core expenses. Families reached a point where they really couldn't save, they turned to credit, and the credit industry has drained billions of dollars out of their pockets. So, it's going to take time to rebuild the middle class, and that really is part of the problem. (Morgan, 2010)

Indeed, as the CFPB Chief indicated, the return to inequality has been a 20-25 year trend, but, unlike the national inequality before the Great Depression, the current one is much easier to document. The government now keeps very good records, and the numbers tell the story. The U.S. Census data clearly verifies that the top echelons are getting richer and richer at the expense of the rest of America. Table 14-1 indicates the percentages of Americans' income that different wage ranges control.

Table 14-1:

Population	Income Range	Share of Country's Income
Lowest fifth	less than $20,453	3.4
Second fifth	$20,454 – 38,550	8.6
Middle fifth	38,551 – 61,801	14.6
Fourth fifth	61,802 – 100,000	23.2
Highest fifth	100,000 and above	50.3

(U.S. Census Bureau, Current Population Reports: Income, Poverty, and Health Insurance in the United States, 2009)

Hence, the top 20% of America's population, those earning $100,000 or more, control a majority of the nation's income.

But, how does the above data compare to past years, i.e. what is the trend? Again, we turn to government records. Looking at several selected years of quintile percentages, Table 14-2 yields:

Table 14-2

	Share of Country's Income				
	1969	1979	1989	1999	2009
Lowest quintile	4.1	4.1	3.8	3.6	3.4
Second quintile	10.9	10.2	9.5	8.9	8.6
Middle quintile	17.5	16.8	15.8	14.9	14.6
Fourth quintile	24.5	24.6	24.0	23.2	23.2
Highest quintile	43.0	44.2	46.8	49.4	50.3

(U.S. Census Bureau, Current Population Reports: Income, Poverty, and Health Insurance in the United States, 2009)

As the information clearly shows, the distribution of household income in the lowest to the fourth quintiles; i.e., 80% of the U.S. population has declined over the last 30 years. The top 20% of the population has increased to the point of owning over half of the nation's wealth. And, notice that, since the 4th quintile (households with incomes of $60,000 - $100,000) has essentially remained constant, the growth in the top fifth of the nation's population has been taken from the middle and lower income levels.

One more table may help verify the point. Table 14-3 lists the percentage of households by income ranges.

Table 14-3

Percentage Distribution					
Income Ranges	1969	1979	1989	1999	2009
Less than $25,000	27.6	27.1	25.3	23.1	24.9
$25,000 - $49,999	31.0	27.9	26.3	24.9	25.2
$50,000 - $99,999	33.9	34.0	32.5	31.2	29.6
$100,000 - 199,999	6.8	9.8	13.7	16.8	16.3
Over $200,000	0.8	1.2	2.2	4.0	3.8

(U.S. Census Bureau, Current Population Reports: Income, Poverty, and Health Insurance in the United States, 2009)

Again, the data shows that the higher income levels have risen while "middle America" has lost ground.

Comparing only the last 10 years or so, the Center on Budget and Policy Priorities indicated that the average income of the bottom quintile, estimated at $18,116, declined 2.5% since the 1990's, the middle quintile's average income of $50,434 edged up 1.3% since the 1990's, and the top 20% of Americans, whose average income was $132,131, rose by 9% since the 1990's (Lughby, 2008).

So, the pendulum seems to be swinging back to pre-1900 era when America essentially had a two class society. We appear to be seriously heading in that direction again.

Who Cares?

"So what if we have an income gap? Isn't America the land of opportunity where anyone is entitled to become a millionaire if possible? If others can't hack it or can't figure it out, that's their problem? A growing income gap just sounds like a few have worked harder or smarter than the rest, and they are enjoying the fruit of their labors. If a two class society develops, so be it. Who cares? That's how capitalism works sometimes."

Have you heard someone express similar sentiments in your life? Yes, most notably, Mitt Romney.

The issue here, of course, is one of equity, and recall that equity is not the same as equality. Again, Americans aren't clamoring for all to have the same outcome—equal incomes—as Americans acknowledge that there are indeed a variety of reasons why different citizens will receive different incomes. But, citizens, especially American citizens, believe that there ought to be a reasonable connection between one's diligence and hard work and the ability to acquire enough wealth to enjoy a decent standard of living. That notion regards a sense of fairness, i.e. equity.

But, if that connection (between legitimate effort and positive outcome) begins to erode or evaporate because others are able to "hog" a share that is far above a reasonable connection, resentment and social upheaval can develop. Employees who serve as teachers, fire fighters, accountants, nurses, social workers, car mechanics, biologists, and on and on will question why hedge fund executives or athletes or movie and television stars or Fortune 500 CEOs work so much harder or better to be entitled to such staggering sums. And, certainly, millions of Americans question the ethics of businesses paying its managers high salaries and/ or granting million dollar bonuses to a top manager while also laying off their direct line workers and/or outsourcing their labor forces.

So, while no one contends that laziness should ever be defended or accommodated, there is a sense of reasonableness and equity at stake. Motivation matters, and it is important to social harmony that most people believe they will be able to take care of themselves and their families if they exert diligence and dedication. But, they also believe that they should be able to provide on par with others who have similar work ethics, skills, and educational backgrounds.

Fairness is the heart of the matter.

Public Policy Implications

At the turn of the 20th century, it was apparent that the U.S. had a large gap between the "haves" and the "have-nots," but it was believed that, while unfortunate, there wasn't anything that could be done about it. Prompted by the Great Depression and World War II, increased governmental involvement in the economy pretty much proved that belief to be wrong. While one may be philosophically opposed to significant government intervention, it certainly seems feasible that a country can "create" and/or enhance a thriving middle class - if it truly wishes to do so. The real question, then, is whether the country has the will to do so. And, I suppose, an immediate follow-up question is how might that income inequality be reduced? (The devil is in the details, as they say.)

If the United States decides that it truly wants to have a (large) middle class, then there is no getting around it: some income and wealth redistribution will need to take place; not overnight, but a new trend line will need to be facilitated. "The lesson of history is that, in the long run, super-elites have two ways to survive: by suppressing dissent or by sharing their wealth" (Freeland, 2011). Politics is how economic priorities are set, and the excessively wealthy will not likely go down without a political fight. However, assuming 90% of the population can ignore their differences on other issues and band together on this one, there are steps that can be taken to "force" the top 10% to begin sharing their wealth. (Or, if some will prefer to donate sums for needed projects, "forcing" can be tempered.)

But, certainly, one should start with taxes, and there are a host of specific changes (some are loopholes) that should be addressed. It may very well be that America's general tax code needs to be reformed and simplified, but we also need to target certain tax policies that will help redistribute wealth. So, first, the marginal tax rate for those at the top could be increased. Second, the capital gains rate could also be raised, or change the way certain types of income are classified (e.g. hedge fund income). Third, we could prevent American corporations from sending profits to overseas locations where tax rates are lower.

Second, we need to "trade" a better work ethic for reasonable safety net provisions for those that are diligent, but incur unfortunate circumstances. Most Americans rightfully complain about the entitlement mentality that has developed over the last few decades, and that must be vigorously addressed. Most Americans, whether Christian or not, tend to believe that the Bible, if nothing else, is an excellent manual for living, and the scriptures clearly suggest that those who aren't willing to work don't eat (II Thessalonians 3:6-13). And what about, "Blessed are the poor for theirs is the kingdom of heaven?" And, the "T" in TANF's welfare reform in the 1990's needs to be stressed: welfare benefits are to be temporary for the truly needy. But students will ask," So if you have a lifelong disability which truly prevents you from working—either congenital or acquire—we should just put you out to die?" What good are "temporary benefits" for these people? But, in exchange for a national commitment to individual responsibility, we should also increase the earned income tax credit, provide efficient food and shelter assistance to the truly destitute, and provide child care assistance to single parents who seek to get an education or work in a low paying job.

Third, we need a renewed effort to assist employees in forming a union if properly pursued and elected. It is unclear whether increased union formation would yield better wages for employees, but they can serve as a counterbalance for promoting workplace safety, improving human resource practices, and establishing more ethical promotion and termination procedures.

Fourth, while America may never wish to adopt a European style socialism, we could then craft our own "managed" capitalism in which we collectively provide two rather basic components to a thriving middle class: universal health care and a minimum retirement program. We are currently engaged in a rather heated debate about whether (nearly) all American citizens will have some health insurance coverage, and if so, how will it be provided and paid for, and no one quite knows as of this writing how it will turn out. But, clearly, if the free market could be relied on to provide the affordable solutions we need, there would never have been any reform attempts in the first place. It appears that some combination of free market and government regulation will be needed. To promote a solid middle class, such health insurance must provide coverage for everyone (with no exemptions for pre-existing conditions) at a cost that most can afford (and financial assistance for those unable to afford it). But, we need to cover all.

And, while the Social Security system is also under fire (mostly because the average life expectancy has dramatically increased in the last 50 years), some sort of publicly financed minimum retirement plan is needed. Americans need to save more, in general, and they need to be taught to invest in retirement plans, in particular, but a retirement floor will aid in maintaining a solid middle class.

Lastly, while seemingly radical, some have renewed the notion of an annual income cap (Dietl, H., Duschl, T. and Lang, M., 2010). the most jolting idea that deserves a great deal of public debate is that of an annual income cap. One way to allow middle and lower class wages to increase is to prevent top incomes from raking so much off the top, i.e. put a limit on how much income one may earn in a year's period of time. To fight inflation, President Nixon froze wages and prices for a year in the 1970's, and one of the first acts that President Obama undertook when he was elected in 2008 was to issue an Executive Order that capped wages for all federal government employees at $350,000 per year, and he subsequently "jawboned" for CEO compensation to be limited to $500,000 a year to those American firms, mostly banks, that received bail-out loans. The idea is not new, Hence. And, President Obama reduced his own salary, Obama reduced his own pay.

What if the ,for instance, instituted an annual cap of $1,000,000.00 ? Yes, the 1% of our population that earns larger sums would squawk, and other "well-to-do" folks who have hopes of earning that ceiling would equally balk at such a limitation. But, why should the vast majority of Americans have any serious objection? (To be sure, many Americans still dream of becoming a millionaire, but the odds are extremely low.) talented could still be well-compensated, and such compensation could occur year after year (after year, etc.); but the cap would help make funds available to be "spread around" a bit to others who also work hard at providing important jobs in our economy.

Or, here's another option proffered by some economists: put a cap on the ratio of top employee compensation to low employee compensation. What does that mean? In the 1950's the top manager in an American company received compensation that was about 25 times more than the compensation paid to the company's low level worker. In the 1980's that ratio had grown to 40 times, and in the 1990's, average CEO pay was 100 times the pay of the direct line worker. Today, that ratio is over 350 times. Again, using GM and Wal-Mart as examples, the General Motors' CEO in 1968 was paid $4 million which was 66 times what the assembly line worker earned, but in 2005, Wal-Mart's CEO was paid $17.5 million, which was 900 times what the average Wal-Mart employee made (Reich, 2007). Another strategy might be to place a limit on what the ratio can be between the highest paid employee (typically the top manager) and the lowest.

Admittedly, some/many of these notions seem anti-American, although many think that paying someone millions of dollars a year to sing, throw a ball, or make excessively risky investments is rather un-American as well. Indeed, one's personal values and priorities will pretty much shape whether the current income gap bothers you and/or whether you believe the country should do anything about it. Problems and their possible solutions are inherently full of value judgments.

But, the data is unambiguous; America is on its way to a very real two-class society, with the majority falling into the "lower" class. Doing nothing will most assuredly create more and more social tension and possible disorder. If we wish to regain a meaningful middle class, we must do something. Trends don't change course on their own, so, if nothing else, perhaps this chapter can serve to stimulate your thinking and some subsequent discussion.

▶▶ *Chapter 14 Review*

Key concepts:

1. The United States is been experiencing a growing income gap for the past 20+ years.

2. America also experienced a significant income inequality between the Civil War and the Great Depression, but the United States created a "middle class" during the period of the 1950's, 1960's, 1970's, and 1980's.

3. The United States government took specific steps to establish the middle class, prompted mostly by the Great Depression and World War II.

4. Data from the mid-1980's onward confirm a trend of an ever increasing gap between the "haves" and the "have-nots."

5. The growing income gap is likely to continue (and possibly threaten social cohesion) unless steps are taken to reverse the trend. Some steps might include:

    a. Change marginal tax rates on the upper income brackets; change capital gain tax rates and close a capital gains loophole that benefits hedge funds

    b. Promote messages of increased individual responsibility, but also provide meaningful financial assistance to the truly needy

    c. Allow unions to properly and legally form

    d. Provide a universal health care plan that acceptably combines free enterprise with government oversight; provide a retirement assistance program (e.g. acceptably reform Social Security)

    e. Limit excessive annual incomes

6. The author hopes the chapter will at least facilitate some critical thinking and ongoing discussion.

REFERENCES

Aversa, J. (2010), *Bernanke takes defense of Fed to '60 Minutes'*, Retrieved at http://www.msnbc.com/id/40522301/ns/business-eye_on_the-economy/ on 12/5/2010

Barro, R. (2010), *The Folly of Subsidizing Unemployment*, Retrieved at http://online.wsj.com/article/SB1000142405274870395970457545443145772018 8.html on 9/3/2010

Bartiromo, M. (2010), *The week that changed wall street*, New York, Penguin Publishing

Blackstone, B. & Walker, M. (2011), *Global Price Fears Mount*, Retrieved ay http://online.wsj.com/article/SB100014240527487033985045760996802 69779402.html?mod=djem_jiewr_EM_domainid on 1/28/2011

Bureau of Labor Statistics, Labor Force Statistics from the Current Population Survey, *Civilian labor force participation rate*, Retrieved from http://www.data.bls.gov on 10/15/2010

Bureau of Labor Statistics, Labor Force Statistics from the Current Population Survey, *Unemployment rate 16 years and over*, Retrieved from http://www.data.bls.gov on 10/15/2010

Bureau of Labor Statistics, *Working in the 21st Century, Labor force participation rates by gender*, Retrieved from http://www.bls.gov/opub/working/chart3.pdf on 10/15/2010

Coy, P. (2010) The future of Fannie and Freddie, *Business Week*, July 28, 2008

Federal Reserve of Minneapolis, *Consumer Price Index 1913 -*, Retrieved from http://www.minneapolisfed.org/community_education/teacher/calc/hist1913.cfm on 12/03/2010

Federal Reserve, *Map of Federal Reserve Banks*, Retrieved from http://www.federalreserve.gov/gifjpg/lastmap2.gif on 11/29/2919

Financial Crisis Inquiry Commission, *Financial Crisis Inquiry Commission Releases Report on the Causes of the Financial Crisis*, Retrieved at http://www.fcic.gov/files/news_pdfs/2011-0127-fcic-releases-report.pdf on 1/28/2011

Freeland, C. (2011). The Rise of the New Global Elite, *The Atlantic, January/February 2011*

Fullerton, H. & Tossi, M, *Labor force projections to 2010: steady growth and changing composition*, Monthly Labor Review, November, 2001

Gordon, M. (2010), *"Ex-CEO: Market forces killed Bear Stearns"*, Retrieved at http://www.msnbc.msn.com/id/36958429/ns/business-us_business/ on 5/5/2010

Gross, D. (2010 What Government Takeover? Retrieved at http://www.newsweek.com/id/234745/output/print on 3/11/2010

Hilsenrath, J. (2010), *Central Bank Treads Into Once-Taboo Realm*, Retrieved at http://online.wsj.com/article/SB100014240527487048052045755948330 95922308.html on 11/15/2010

Hope, Y. (9/28/2010) *Income Gap Between Rich, Poor the Widest Ever*, Retrieved from http://www.cbsnews.com on 10/13/2010

InflationData.com, (2010) *Current Consumer Price Index*, Retrieved at http://www.inflationdata.com/Inflation/Consumer-Price_Index/CurrentCPI.asp on 11/26/2020

Internal Revenue Service, *S Corporations*, Retrieved from http://www.irs.gov/business/small/article/0,,id=98263,00.html on 6/26/2010

Izzo, P. (2011) *Economists Optimistic on Growth*, Retrieved at http://www.wsj.com/article/SB10001424052748704307404576079870784741108.html?mod=dj on 1/21/2011

Johnston, D. (3/29/2007). *Income Gap Is Widening, Data Shows*, Retrieved from http://www.nytimes.com on 10/13/2010

Krantz, M. (2010), *Worries outweigh profits reports*, USA Today, July 30,2010

Krugman, P, Wells, R. & Olney, Martha (2007). *Essential of economics*, New York, Worth Publishers

Krugman, P. (2007). *The Conscience of a liberal*, New York, W.W. Norton & Company

Lahart, J. (2011) *Companies Cling to Cash*, Retrieved at http://online.wsj.com/article/SB100014240527448703766704576009501161973480.html?mod=dj on 1/24/2011

Lazzaro, J. (2011) *Will the Economic Recovery Slide on $90 Oil?*, Retrieved at http://www.dailyfinance.com/story/will-90-oil-jeopardize-economic-recovery/19808358/on 1/23/2011

Lee, M & Mather, M. (2008). Population Bulletin, U.S. Labor Force Trends, Vol 63, No 2, p 5-6.

Levi, M. (1981). *Economics deciphered*, New York, Basic Books, Inc. Publishers

Lieber, R. & Siegel Barnard, T. (2010), *From Card Fees to Mortgages, a New Day for Consumers*, Retrieved at http://www.nytimes.com/2010/06/26/your-money/26money.html on 6/25/2010

Luhby, T. (4/9/2008) *As income gap widens, recession fears grow*, Retrieved from http://www.cnnmoney on 1/14/2009

Maltby, E. (2010), *Collateral Damage in Lending*, Retrieved at http://online.wsj.com/article/SB10001424052748703792704575366992490339102.html on 8/2/2010

Mastrianna, F. (2008). *Basic economics*, (14th edition), Mason, South-West Cengage Learning

McEachern,W. (2000). *Economics: a contemporary introduction*, (5th edition), Cincinnati, South-Western College Publishing

McKinnon, J. (2010) *U.S. Weighs Tax That Has VAT of Political Trouble*, Retrieved at http://online.wsj.com/article/SB10001424052748704799604575357311577610390.html on 7/16/2010

McLean, B. & Nocera, J. (2010). *All the devils are here*, New York, Portfolio/Penguin

McLaughlin, M. (1999) *Clinton, Republicans agree to deregulation of US financial system*, Retrieved from http://www.wsws.org/articles/1999/nov1999/bank-n01.shtml on 11/28/2009

McMahon, T. *Historical CPI-U data from 1913 to the present*, Retrieved from http://inflationdata.com on 12/03/2010

Moneychimp, *Components of the Gross Domestic Product*, Retrieved at http://www.moneychimp.com/articles/econ/gdp_diagram.htm on 7/1/2010

Morgenson, G. Untangling the Complex Foreclosure Mess, National Public Radio's Fresh Air Program, Retrieved on http://www.npr.org/templates/story/story.php?storyId=130835119 on 10/28/2010

Morgan, D. (9/21/10). *Warren: Middle Class Has Suffered for 30 Years*, Retrieved at http://www.cbsnews.com on 12/15/2010

MSNBC.com (2010) *5 weeks on the brink: Reliving the meltdown*, Retrieved at http://www.msnbc.msn.com/id/32733642/ns/business-stocks_and_economy/ on 9/14/2009

Murray, S. (2010) *Long Recession Ignites Debate on Jobless Benefits*, Retrieved at http://online.wsj.com/article/SB100014240527487043346045753386919139948 92.htmlOn 7/16/2010

Murray, S. (2010) *Slump Over, Pain Persists*, Retrieved at http://online.wsj.com/article/SB10001424052748703989304575503691644231892.html on 9/24/2010

Newport, F. (2009), *Americans Split on Redistributing Wealth by Taxing the Rich*, Retrieved from http://www.gallop.com on 11/17/2009

Occupational Outlook Quarterly, *Labor force*, Winter 2005-06, p 47-50

Peter G. Peterson Foundation, *IOUSA Solutions* (video), Retrieved at http://www.pgpf.org/Media/Video/2010/09/iousa-solutions.aspx on 12/27/2010

Price Waterhouse Coopers (2010), What makes a good tax system?, Retrieved at http://www.pwc.com/gx/en/paying-taxes/good-tax-system.jhtml on 5/10/2010

Reich, R. (2007). Supercapitalism, New York, Alfred A. Knopf

Reddy, S. (2010), *GDP Grows Too Slowly to Fill Job Gaps*, Retrieved at http://online.wsj.com/article/SB1000142405270230415560457558198164432592 8.htmlon 11/05/2010

Ruffing, K. & Horney, J. (2010), *Where Today's Large Deficits Come From*, Retrieved at http://www.cbpp.org/cms/index.cfm?fa=view&id=3036 on 5/10/2010

Schultz, G. et al (2010), *Principles for Economic Revival*, Retrieved at http://online.wsj.com/article/SB1000142405274870346670457548983004163350 8.html on 9/24/2010

Schumman, J. (2010) *How a Poorer America Is Holding Back the Recovery*, Retrieved at http://www.aolnews.com/2010/09/16/how-a-poorer-america-is-holding-back-the-recovery/ on 9/17/2010

Shell, E. (2010), *Fed to Engage in Second Round of Quantitative Easing*, Retrieved at http://www.pbs.org/newshour/rundown/2010/11/fed-slow-growth-disappointing-will-engage-in-second-round-of-quantitiative-easing.html# on 11/3/2010

Taylor, A. (2010), *Deficit-cut plan fails to advance to Capitol*, Retrieved on http://www.msnbc.com/id/40489484/ns/politics-capitol_hill/ on 12/03/2010

Taylor, J (2011), *A Two-Track Plan to Restore Growth*, Retrieved at http://online. wsj.com/article/SB10001424052748704268104576107951413818460. html?mod=WSJ_newsreel_opinion#printMode on 1/28/2011

U.S. Census Bureau, *Current Population Reports: Income, Poverty, and Health Insurance Coverage in the United States: 2009*, Issued September 2010

Wall Street Journal (2011). *Obama's Rule-Making Loophole*, Retrieved at http:// online.wsj.com/article/SB1000142405274870488130457609413289686258 2.html?mod=djem_jiewr_EC_domainid on 1/28/2011

Weisberg, J. (2010), *What Caused the Economic Crisis?*, Retrieved at http://www. slate.com/toolbar.aspx?action=print&id=22440858 on 10/11/2010

Weisman, J. (2010), *Economic Policy "Nudge" Givs Way to a Shove*, Retrieved at http://online.wsj.com/article/SB1000142405274870486930457510398023 2739138.html on 3/12/2010

GLOSSARY

Absolute advantage: the ability to produce more output using the same amount of resources; the ability to produce the same output using fewer resources

Bank: a business that receives savings from the general public and re-routes those funds into lending and/or investment opportunities; commercial banks engage in traditional lending activities in which a borrower is expected to repay a loan, while investment banks use customer deposits to purchase stock, bonds, real estate, and other investments

Bank run: many customers opt to withdraw their deposits/close their accounts rather simultaneously, usually due to a real or rumored fear that the bank is about to close

Barter: two parties agree to exchange services or finished goods of alleged equal value

Bonds: essentially a formalized I.O.U.; Party loans money to Party B, and Party B promises to repay the entire sum plus a stipulated amount of interest by a specified date

Breakeven point: the number of units a business must sell so that its revenue at that volume equals its costs at that volume; no profit, but also no loss

Capital: money; capital can also mean equipment or machinery used to produce other goods

Capitalism: an economic system that emphasizes individual decision-making; a market driven system in which buyers and sellers freely determine what goods and services are produced, who will produce them, and who will receive them

Command economy: an economic system in which a governmental authority makes decisions about the production and consumption of goods and services

Commercial bank: see bank

Communism: an economic system that emphasizes group decision-making; a command economy in which a government al authority makes the decisions about production and consumption of goods and services.

Comparative Advantage: the ability to produce at a lower opportunity cost

Consumer Price Index (CPI): a measurement of the changes in the prices of goods and services over time

Consumer sovereignty: consumers (customers) decide what products and services are to be produced in an economy

Corporation: a legal form of business ownership in which the owners are protected from unlimited liability

Demand/Demand Curve: a graph that pictures the inverse relationship between price levels and quantity levels that consumers will buy; if the price of good increases, chances is high that consumers will buy less, and if the price of good decreases, chances is high that consumers will buy more

Demand shift: quantity levels that consumers will buy – at all price levels – can increase or decrease (shift) because of special developments such as fads, income adjustments, or future expectations

Discount rate: the interest rate that the Federal Reserve charges banks who borrow from it

Economics: the study of how a group makes choices to use scarce resources

EFT (Electronic Fund Transfer): a modern age form of money in which payments (income and bills) are made electronically via computers

Elasticity: the measurement of responsiveness by consumers to changes in prices by sellers

Equilibrium: the price level at which the quantity supplied by sellers equals the quantity demanded by consumers; no shortage and no surplus

Excise tax: taxes that are targeted to a particular item, e.g. cigarettes, gasoline, yachts

Export: a product made domestically is sold abroad

Federal Deposit Insurance Corporation (FDIC): an independent agency, funded by premiums paid by private banks that monitors the financial health of banks and insures deposits up to $250,000 per account

Federal Reserve System (the FED): the central bank of the U.S. whose role is to monitor/control the country's money supply

Fiat money: money that has value because the government has "decreed it so"

Fiscal policy: the government's right to tax and spend

Fixed cost: a business expense that does not change as the business' sales volume changes

Free enterprise: an economic system in which the means of production are privately owned for the purpose of making profit; activities are controlled more by market forces than government planning

Frictional (unemployment): unemployment that occurs because the employee voluntarily quit

Gross Domestic Product (GDP): the measurement of economic activity and economic growth

Import: a product made abroad is sold domestically

Inflation: a persistent increase in the average price level of the country's goods and services

Injection: funds that "leak" out of the economy's circular flow are put back in; injections regard loans, government spending, and exports

Interest: the cost of borrowing, i.e. the sum paid by the borrower when receiving a loan

Investment bank: see bank

Labor force: the number of people who are working plus those who are unemployed and looking for work

Laissez faire: a French phrase literally meaning "let it be" or "let it alone"; a laissez faire economy is one in which the government has next to no involvement

Leakage: funds that drop out of the economy's circular flow; leaks regard savings, taxes, and imports

Legal reserve requirement: the percentage of customer's deposits that banks must keep in reserve, i.e. not loan

Legal tender: forms of money that creditors must allow debtors to use in satisfying their obligations; coins and currency are legal tender, while the acceptability of other common forms of payments are determined by individual sellers (some businesses accept checks and some do not, for example)

Limited Liability Corporation (LLC): allowed by state statutes, a business structure that seeks to provide some personal liability protection to business owners

M1 (and M2 and M3): measurements of money in the money supply; M1 = coins, currency, checking accounts, and travelers checks/money orders; M2 = M1 plus savings accounts and short term investment accounts; M3 = M2 plus long term investment accounts

Macroeconomics: the "big picture" subjects of economics such as economic growth, aggregate production, general price levels, inflation, and employment

Marginal cost: the extra expense of producing one more unit

Marginal revenue: the extra sum gained by selling one more units

Marginal utility: the amount of extra pleasure or satisfaction gained by consuming one more units

Market driven economy: an economy in which the basic decisions about production, distribution, and consumption are determined by voluntary, individual judgments of buyers and sellers

Market structure: the fundamental features of a collection of businesses that form an industry that include the number of firms, the uniqueness of the product, the influence on pricing, and the ease of entry or exit

Medicaid: a government sponsored health care program for the poor

Medicare: a government sponsored health care program for the elderly

Medium of exchange: any tangible item that facilitates a transaction; money is defined as a medium of exchange because the coin, paper, gem, plastic, etc. aid in the transaction of business

Microeconomics: the "particular picture" of economic issues of specific categories of individuals, firms, and industries

Minimum Wage: legislation that requires businesses to pay covered employees at least a specific amount

Monetary policy: regulation of the country's money supply to affect general price levels and interest rates

Money: anything that is widely accepted as payment for desired goods and services

Monopoly: a business that is the only provider of a product/service that has no close substitute

Monopolistic competition: a market structure that has ample competition with products that is unique enough to justify differing prices

Multiplier Effect: the "rippling" consequence of an initial autonomous expenditure

Oligopoly: a market structure with few competitors who are usually interdependent

Open Market Transactions: the FED buys and sells bonds

Opportunity cost: the value of the next best option that is given up when a choice is made

Paradox of Thrift: an increase in aggregate savings, usually a good thing, will likely cause a significant contraction in spending, which will, in turn, lead to layoffs, i.e. unemployment, a bad thing

Perfect competition: a market structure that has too many competitors with products that are not unique enough to justify differing prices; firms are "price takers" cannot sell at higher prices

Price elasticity: see elasticity

Production function: a table that shows the relationship between inputs and resulting outputs at different levels of capacity

Production Possibility Frontier (Curve): a picture that depicts the output achievable when all production resources are used; it also shows the trade-offs a country faces between alternative goods and services

Profit: revenue minus expenses; it is also the typical incentive that entrepreneurs have for starting a business

Progressive tax: a tax in which the burden of the tax is higher on people with higher incomes

Proportional tax: a tax in which the burden of the tax is the same for all levels of income

Quantity Theory of Money: a theory that suggests that changing the quantity of money in the money supply with consequently change the price level

Regressive tax: a tax in which the burden of the tax is higher on people with lower income

Rent: a fee paid to a landowner for exclusive use of the land for a specific period of time

Savings: income not currently needed for consumption of goods and services

Scarcity: the wants of consumers exceed the available resources to satisfy those wants

Sherman Anti-Trust Act: 1890 legislation aimed at restoring competition and preventing monopolies

Shortage: the demand for a product is higher than the supply of that product

Smith, Adam: the acknowledged founder of capitalism who authored "An Inquiry into the Nature and Causes of the Wealth of Nations" (commonly referred to as "The Wealth of Nations") in 1776

Socialism: an economic system that is a hybrid between capitalism and communism; socialism embraces some significant intervention of government into the country's economic activities while generally encouraging/allowing free enterprise to occur in many/most markets

Social Security: a government sponsored retirement program for the elderly and eligible disabled

Sole Proprietorship: a business that has one owner

Structural (unemployment): unemployment that occurs because the laborer no longer has knowledge or a skill that is valued by the economy

Supply/Supply Curve: a graph that pictures the direct relationship between price levels and quantity levels that consumers will buy; if the price of good increases, chances is high that sellers will provide more, and if the price of good decreases, chances are high that sellers will provide less

Supply shift: quantity levels that sellers will provide – at all price levels – can increase or decrease (shift) because of special developments such as technological innovation, cost changes, or future expectations

Surplus: the supply of a product is higher than the demand for the product

Tax: a governmental levy to raise revenue; taxes are levied on income, sales, property, or any item that politicians decide is appropriate

Unemployment rate: the percentage of the labor force that is unemployed (and looking for work)

Unemployment benefits: a governmental program to provide a modest income to lay off workers while they presumably search for new employment

Utility: pleasure or satisfaction

Variable cost: a business expense that does change as the business' sales volume changes; examples include inventory or raw materials

COURSE LAYOUT

I teach an economics course called American Free Enterprise, both in a traditional classroom and in an online platform, in an adult accelerated degree program. If this may help you organize your course, I use the following course layout:

	On ground		Online	
Week	Topics	Textbook	Topics	Resources*
1	Introd. & syllabus 3 basic queries 3 econ systems GDP/Circular Flow Leakages/injections	Ch 1-3	Introductions 3 basic queries 3 econ systems GDP/Circular Flow Leakages/injections	Ch 1-3
2	Supply/Demand Econ goals Legal Bsns Forms Worldviews**	Ch 4-5	Supply/Demand Econ goals Legal Bsns Forms Worldviews**	Ch 4-5
3	Quiz #1 Fiscal policy Price Elasticity Paper #1	Ch 11 & Ch 6	Quiz #1 Fiscal Policy Price elasticity Paper #1	Ch 11 & Ch 6
4	Marginal Util Prod Func. (MR=MC) Break even point	Ch 6 & Ch 8	Marginal Util Prod Func (MR=MC) Break even point	Ch 6 & Ch 8
5	Quiz #2 Market structures Competition v stewardship*** Paper #2	Ch 7	Quiz #2 Market structures Competition/stewardship*** Paper #2	Ch 7
6	Money & Banking Fed Reserve System Monetary v fiscal policies	Ch 9-10	Money & banking Fed Reserve System Monetary v fiscal policies	Ch 9-10
7	Unemployment Inflation Income dist. Inequality Public policy	Ch 12 - Ch 14	Unemployment Inflation Income dist. inequality Public policy	Ch 12- Ch 14
8	Quiz #3 Team Paper/Presentations	Quiz #3	Team Paper/Presentations****	

- Resources in an online course can also include videos, PPT, chat rooms, et al

**   Worldviews is a discussion about various philosophical mindsets which can be ignored or replaced with another topic an instructor deems more valuable

***   Waste management can still be a worthwhile economic discussion, but Stewardship is specifically included in my classes at a Christian university

****   Online group presentations are handled via PPT in the "live chat" feature of the online platform